Thank  ... ministry! I pray this book blesses you & you

Daily WORD

you see and expirence the Lords blessings first hand! He loves you! God Bless, Kayla

KAYLA HAYHURST

All scripture quotations, unless otherwise indicated, are taken from the *Holy Bible, King James Version. KJV.* Public Domain.

All word definitions are from Dictionary.com.

FIRST EDITION

ISBN: 978-0-9970518-6-5

Library of Congress Control Number: 2016935479

Published by

Certa
PUBLISHING

P.O. Box 2839, Apopka, FL 32704

Printed in the United States of America

Acknowledgements

$\mathcal{I}$ thank Jesus Christ my Lord, Savior, Friend, Father, Redeemer, Author, Comforter, and so much more — my everything — for using me as a vessel for Him to work through. I give all the credit to Jesus because He did it all.

I thank my husband, Timmy, who the Lord placed in my life to encourage me to not give up. When I prayed to have a greater desire to be in His Word, the Lord answered my prayer by giving me the desire to write this devotional. I told my husband about it. At that point, we didn't have a computer or internet. On Valentine's Day I woke up to a table set with everything I needed, including the Word, to get started on my writing journey. He pushes me to seek all that God has for me. Thank you for your support. I love you.

To my sister-in-law, Codi — if you had not been obedient in writing your study guide first, I wouldn't have thought it possible for me to start my devotional. It is important in life to have a Christian mentor to lead, guide, and direct you in the ways of the Lord. You have been that for me.

To my sister-in-law, Cassi — you are an example of what a Godly woman should be. I thank God for having you both as amazing examples to follow in the Lord.

To my mother, Pam — the Lord has given me such an amazing mother, who went without at times just so I could be blessed. You are the best person I know. Thank you for encouraging me every step of the way, for all your prayers, and always making me feel that I can accomplish anything through the Lord. God knew what He was doing when He placed you as my mother. Then God gave me another mother when I got married. Jenni, I am so thankful that God placed me in your family. He knew we would make a perfect match. You're more than a mother-in-law; you're like a best friend that encourages me in everything I do and always reminds me to "not let the devil steal my joy."

To my church family, you are the theme throughout this book. You are the reason I have anything to write. Each and every one of you will see yourselves in this book. Thank you for helping me grow in the Lord. I thank Jesus for placing all of you in my life, helping me grow in Him. Todd King, my pastor — thank you for going above and beyond and being an example of how to serve Jesus inside and outside of church.

To my family — thank you for encouraging me, always loving me, and never giving up on me. I thank all of you for taking me to church when I was younger. I'm thankful for the Word always being available and for a family that always talked about it and was a living example of it. Thank you for teaching me the ways of the Lord. Bri - thank you for all your love, encouragement, and support always.

To my friends — thank you for your support and interest in this book. Your interest, and asking me questions, and support was so encouraging. I thank Matt Murry for participating in my events and asking questions. You were one of the first people that sought me out and asked questions, showing an interest in my writing. I am so thankful for that. Thank you all for your continued interest, and encouragement.

To Certa Publishing — Sheila and Jennifer — thank you for working with me and making God's plan come to life. You are a blessing.

Thank you Pookie Hayhurst, my little Dachshund who sat on my lap for the entire writing of this book, keeping me warm, and showing me love every day.

How to Use This Devotional

This is a "hands-on" devotional, set up so that you can easily remember your devotions. The problem with most devotions is, we read it and then forget it because they are so long. This devotion is a daily word that you have to remember—just one word, which will then trigger the rest of the devotion for that day. Each page has a word that starts with the month you are in. The page is written around the daily word. The Lord wants us to daily remember Him and His Word throughout the day.

The Lord put a desire in my heart to write this book. This desire was confirmed when the Lord told me to talk to a particular man in our church. I don't normally talk to this man about things, but the Lord said he had the answer. I, nervously, walked up to him and began talking to him about my desire to write a daily devotional. He looked at me and said, "Sometimes we miss opportunities because we sit around and wait. Sometimes we need big confirmations. So if you can answer 'yes' to both of these questions, do it with all of your might: "Will it bring God glory? Will it draw people to the Lord?" I knew then I had my confirmation. He didn't know what a big confirmation he was for me. I knew the Lord wanted me to do this.

Now, I ask you: Why wouldn't the Lord want you to do this devotional, too? This book will change your life, and it will draw people to the Lord because they will see the change in you. It will bring God glory. So take this step, commit to the Lord, and take this yearlong journey with me. You can start any day and anytime. Every day learn and remember your daily word. Let it impact your life and the lives of those around you. Most importantly, let all you do bring praise to the Lord. Don't miss the opportunity to daily remember the Word.

Kayla

Becoming a Christian

*I*f you are not sure you're a Christian, you came to the right place. Will you accept God's invitation to save you today?

John 3:16 — *For God so loved the world, that he gave his only begotten Son, that whosoever believeth in him should not perish, but have everlasting life.*

Pray this prayer with me:

*J*esus, I know I'm a sinner. I know you paid the price for my sins, and that your blood covers the sins of the world. I know you died on the cross and that you rose again, and that you live today. Jesus, please come into my heart and save my soul. I believe that everything you did, you did for me. Save my soul, Jesus. I love you and I ask you now to put a desire in my heart to serve you fully every day from this moment on. Help me to grow in you. Thank you for the price you paid. Thank you for saving me. Thank you Jesus.

Scriptures that assure your salvation:

Romans 3:23

Romans 6:23

Romans 4:25

Romans 10:9

Romans 10:13

John 1:1

Galatians 2:20

1 John 4:19

JESUS

January 1

Jesus: Gave His life for you on the cross at Calvary. Defeated death. Set you free from sin. Gave you eternal life.

> **Revelation 1:8** — *I am Alpha and Omega, the beginning and the ending, saith the Lord, which is, and which was, and which is to come, the Almighty.*

Testimony

The Lord uses us when we think we are unusable. He loves us when we think we are unlovable. He calls us into a relationship with Him and sets us apart for His glory. The Lord called me when I wouldn't have called myself. I was living a life full of sin, but Jesus saw me through the eyes of His cross and had great plans for me. He will do the same for you.

Mission

> Jeremiah 33:3 — *"Call unto me, and I will answer thee, and shew thee great and mighty things, which thou knowest not."* All you have to do is call.

Daily Notes: _____

_____

_____

_____

_____

_____

_____

_____

JEZEBEL

January 2

Jezebel: was a scheming and shamelessly evil woman. The wife of Ahab, king of Israel: she fostered the worship of Baal and tried to destroy the prophets of Israel (I Kings 18:4–13); she was killed by Jehu (II Kings 9:29–37)

> **2 Kings 9:30** — *And when Jehu was come to Jezreel, Jezebel heard of it; and she painted her face, and tied her head, and looked out at a window.*

Testimony

When Jezebel was about to be killed, her final moments were spent making sure her appearance looked good. After she was killed, the dogs ate her flesh until her appearance became unrecognizable. How much are you counting on your appearance to help you in life? In your eternal life, your appearance doesn't matter. The appearance of others won't affect their eternal life either. Don't be a Jezebel and live your life consumed with your appearance.

Mission

Show others less of you and more of Jesus. Pray for people to be able to see Jesus in you.

Daily Notes: _____

_____

_____

_____

_____

_____

_____

JEZREEL

January 3

Jezreel: ancient Israelite city.

2 Kings 9:17 — *And there stood a watchman on the tower in Jezreel; for he spied the company of Jehu as he came, and said, I see a company. And Joram said, Take a horseman, and send to meet them, and let him say, Is it peace?*

Testimony

Jesus is our strong tower. We can find peace in Him. A tower is used for watching, waiting, and looking. The watchman from the tower could observe whether peace was present in Jezreel or whether there was danger. The question, "Is it peace?" is asked four times throughout the chapter before they got the answer. How many times in your life do you ask yourself "Will this bring me peace?" Jesus is the only one who brings true and ever lasting peace in all circumstances.

Mission

Be a watchman and run to your strong tower. In your tower you don't have to watch, wait, or look for peace. Jesus is your tower and there is an abundance of whatever you need.

Daily Notes: _____

_____

_____

_____

_____

_____

_____

JEHU

January 4

Jehu: a king of Israel noted for his furious chariot attacks. Killed Jezebel.

> **2 Kings 10:15** — *And He said, Come with me, and see my zeal for the Lord. So they made him ride in his chariot.*

Testimony

Jehu claimed to have a zeal for the Lord, but his actions showed otherwise. He was not successful in turning the nation back to the Lord and he tolerated the worshipping of golden calves in the presence of the Lord. Jehu served the Lord halfheartedly. Jehu suffered personally. The nation suffered as well.

Jehu rode in his chariot and was known for his furious chariot attacks. The chariot represents Jehu's heart. He carried his heart everywhere he went, allowing his heart to be attacked by the enemy. Jehu became concerned with only promoting himself rather than the Lord. If he had been serving the Lord wholeheartedly, this wouldn't have happened and Jehu and the nation would not have suffered.

Mission

Give yourself a heart evaluation. Examine yourself in situations, and make sure you are serving the Lord whole-heartedly, and promoting Him above yourself.

Daily Notes: _____

_____

_____

_____

_____

JORAM

January 5

Joram: One of the kings of Israel (2 Kings 8:16, 25, 28). He was the son of Ahab. (2.) Jehoram, the son and successor of Jehoshaphat on the throne of Judah (2 Kings 8:24). Killed by Jehu.

> **2 Kings 8:21** — *So Joram went over to Zair, and all the chariots with him: and he rose by night, and smote the Edomites which compassed him about, and the captains of the chariots and the people fled into their tents.*

Testimony

Later Joram was killed by Jehu in his own chariot. Joram was defeated by the same weapon that he once used to defeat others. He forgot his own battle tactics in fighting the enemy. As a result, he died by a tactic he was familiar with. Don't ever get comfortable with letting the enemy hang around. His strategy is to use your own weapons to defeat you. The end result of letting the enemy win is the same fate as Joram's — death.

Mission

Recognize the weapons in your life to defeat the enemy: praying, attending church, reading the Word, and any other unique way that you can spend time with Jesus. Don't become slack in doing these things. The enemy is always looking for a way to defeat you. Keep your tactics intact.

Daily Notes: _____

_____

_____

_____

_____

JADED

January 6

Jaded: to make or become dull, worn-out, or weary, as from overwork or overuse.

> **Genesis 9:1** — *And God blessed Noah and his sons, and said unto them, be fruitful, and multiply, and replenish the earth.*

Testimony

I'm sure there were times leading up to the flood that Noah felt jaded. Noah was the only person living that found grace with God. So God had him build an ark, which eventually saved him. Noah didn't have the support of people at the time because the world was evil. I'm sure there were many times where Noah had to say to himself, "It's going to flood. It's going to flood."

The Lord had specific instructions for building the ark. The ark had to be built the exact way the Lord instructed so it would withstand the flood. A man without guidance from the Lord might have constantly felt jaded with this impossible job and wouldn't have been able to construct the ark. But Noah found grace for the task because he was a righteous man of God.

Mission

If you think your life is nothing but routine and you're starting to feel jaded, think of Noah and ask God to show you His grace for the task at hand. Routine is not a bad thing when you're in the will of God. After all, it saved Noah and his family's life.

Daily Notes: _____

_____

_____

_____

JUSTIFIED

January 7

Justified: To be just or right. To show a satisfactory reason for something done.

> **Titus 3:7** — *That being justified by his grace, we should be made heirs according to the hope of eternal life.*

Testimony

There is an old hymn that states "I rest my case at the cross." The Bible states we were once lost in sin, but then the love of God appeared to us. Not by the works you've done, but what Jesus did for you and I on the cross. An heir is a person who inherits or has a right of an inheritance following the death of another. Jesus made us heirs to inherit eternal life. We are justified through the death of our Savior on the cross.

Mission

Don't justify yourself. Jesus has already done that for you. Look at yourself today and say "I am justified, satisfied, I have it all. Thank you, Jesus, for settling my case at the cross!"

Daily Notes: _____

_____

_____

_____

_____

_____

_____

_____

JUST

Just: given or awarded rightly; deserved, as a sentence, punishment, or reward:

Romans 1:17 — *for therein is righteousness of God revealed from faith to faith: as it is written, The just shall live by faith.*

Testimony

Paul states that what a believer believes will make a difference. If he believes the gospel, he has life. Otherwise, he has death. Everyone has a chance to believe. Your chance might be right now.

Mission

Don't let yourself feel or let anyone else make you feel like you don't have a right to believe what you do. Jesus gave you the right. You have the right to believe everything Jesus says. Most importantly, everything Jesus says is true and it is for you.

Daily Notes: _____

_____

_____

_____

_____

_____

_____

_____

_____

_____

JUSTIFICATION

Justification: reasonable grounds for complaint, defense,

> **Matthew 4:11** — *Then the devil leaveth him, and, behold the angles came and ministered unto him.*

Testimony

Jesus would have been justified if He defended Himself; but He didn't. Instead He glorified His Father. Jesus went forty days and nights without food. After satan's temptations, the angels came and ministered unto Him. Everything Jesus did, He did for us. He went through every temptation, yet, without sin to help us live. He allowed Himself to be tempted and fought off satan in a beautiful way — with scripture and glorifying His Father.

Mission

When you're looking for reasons for justification, realize who's already won your battle. When you take your eyes off Christ and put it on yourself, satan wins. Don't look for reasonable grounds. Instead, stand on your solid ground — Jesus.

Daily Notes: _____

_____

_____

_____

_____

_____

_____

JUBILE

January 10

Jubile: any season or occasion of rejoicing or festivity.

> **Leviticus 25:12** — *For it is the Jubile; it shall be holy unto you: ye shall eat the increase thereof out of the field.*

Testimony

In Leviticus during the Jubile, the people who bound were set free. The laws were lifted, and people walked in the blessings of the Lord. The people were safe and had plenty to eat. As Christians we all will experience heaven's Jubile on the day the Lord returns. But what about now? How many jubilees are we experiencing in our lives? We have so much to thank the Lord for.

My pastor preached an amazing sermon about a 'good thing' verses a 'God thing.' Just because it's a 'good thing,' doesn't mean it's a 'God thing.' Don't get so comfortable celebrating a 'good thing' that you miss out on a 'God thing.' I don't want anything that's not a God thing. Ask yourself daily is this a good thing; or is this a God thing? Don't miss out on the amazing and incredible God things by settling for the good things in life.

Mission

Start a Jubile in your life. You once were bound, but Jesus set you free. It's a God thing!

Daily Notes: _____

_____

_____

_____

_____

_____

JOY

January 11

Joy: the emotion of great delight or happiness caused by something exceptionally good or satisfying; keen pleasure; elation:

> **1 Peter 1:8** — *Whom having not seen, ye love; in whom, though now ye see him not, yet believing, ye rejoice with joy unspeakable and full of glory:*

Testimony

Jesus died so you could live. Live with joy unspeakable and full of glory. Jesus is always present — no matter what's going on in your life — to give you joy. Satan gives us happiness from time to time and we confuse that with joy. Happiness comes and goes, but joy is forever.

Mission

If you're not experiencing a life full of joy, then remind yourself that Jesus died for you to have joy unspeakable. Pray for that because it's yours.

Daily Notes: _____

_____

_____

_____

_____

_____

_____

_____

_____

_____

JERUSALEM

January 12

Jerusalem: a city in and the capital of Israel: an ancient holy city

> **Matthew 23:37** — *O Jerusalem, Jerusalem, thou that killest the prophets, and stonest them which are sent unto thee, how often would I have gathered thy children together, even as a hen gathereth her chickens under her wings, and ye would not!*

Testimony

How are you responding to people trying to bring you good news? Often times we stone people with our words. Don't take advantage of the "prophets" Jesus has put in your life. Look at their intentions. If they are speaking truth in love towards you to show you Jesus, don't stone them like Jerusalem did.

Mission

Based on this scripture, picture Jesus as a hen and we are all the little chicks under His big, powerful wings. When people spread the truth, remember whose wing you are under and receive it with gladness.

Daily Notes: _____

_____

_____

_____

_____

_____

_____

_____

JEALOUSLY

January 13

Jealously: jealous resentment against a rival, a person enjoying success or advantage; a mental uneasiness from suspicion or fear of rivalry, unfaithfulness

> **Genesis 30:1** — *And when Rachel saw that she bare Jacob no children, Rachel envied her sister; and said unto Jacob, Give me children, or else I die.*

Testimony

Rachel was envious of Leah for having children that she couldn't have. Jesus tells us to not want what others have. Jesus will give us what we need when we need it. We shouldn't look on the things of others, but instead be thankful for what the Lord has given us now. If it isn't God's will for you to have it, then you won't get it until He decides to give it to you.

I bought a beautiful, white vase. I thought of all the different places I was going to sit it in my house. I placed it on the dining room table only to notice the bottom said, "wastebasket." Talk about disappointment! I thought I was getting a good deal on a beautiful vase, which ended up being a wastebasket. That is just like the plans God has for you. Don't settle for the wastebasket when he wants to give you the vase. Don't let jealously force you into the wastebasket kind of life, compared to the beautiful vase God wants you to have.

Mission

When jealousy arrives, think of the wastebasket analogy. Trash is the only thing that goes into a wastebasket. You don't want to waste your life consumed with jealousy, building up trash rather than experiencing what God has for you.

Daily Notes: _____

JACOB

January 14

Jacob: the son of Isaac, twin brother of Esau, and father of the twelve patriarchs of Israel. Husband of Rachel and Leah.

> **Genesis 33:4** — *And Esau ran to meet him and embraced him, and fell on his neck, and kissed him and they wept.*

Testimony

This verse shows us brotherly love. What it doesn't show is the trickery and deceitfulness of Jacob towards Esau. Thanks be to Jesus for having a way to right our wrongs. Jacob was looking for a way to mend things with his brother. Jesus provided.

Mission

If you have a person you've wronged in your life, pray to Jesus for the opportunity to make it right. Jesus will answer. So prepare yourself for the moment. Pray to receive the brotherly love that Jesus calls us to have towards one another.

Daily Notes: _____

_____

_____

_____

_____

_____

_____

_____

_____

_____

JOASH

January 15

Joash: a king of Judah

> **2 Kings 12:2** — *But the high places were not taken away; the people still sacrificed and burned incense in the high places.*

Testimony

Joash was born into evil. Everything around him, including his nation and family, was serving evil. Then Joash became king at the age of 7. He served the Lord. Despite your circumstances you can serve the Lord too.

Mission

No matter what the world and the people in your life are doing, be a Joash and serve the Lord no matter what. Joash was successful and brought glory to God. Live a life that purposes the same.

Daily Notes: _____

_____

_____

_____

_____

_____

_____

_____

_____

_____

_____

JUDGING

January 16

Judging: a person qualified to pass a critical judgment

Matthew 7:1 — *Judge not, that ye be not judged.*

Testimony

We are told to look at ourselves first before criticizing others. By examining ourselves, we get a "reality check" that we have imperfections. The only judging we should do is ourselves. Do we line up with the Word of God? Are we showing others Jesus?

Mission

When you find yourself judging others, look first at yourself and then look to Jesus. Show the ones you're judging the love of Christ.

Daily Notes: _____

_____

_____

_____

_____

_____

_____

_____

_____

_____

_____

_____

_____

JUDGED

January 17

Judged: to hear evidence in a case in order to pass judgment.

Romans 2:13 — *For not the hearers of the laws are just before God, but the doers of the law shall be justified.*

Testimony

Man looks on the outward appearance, but Jesus sees the heart. We are no longer judged according to the law. Jesus pleads our case before the Father because He accomplished everything on the cross.

Mission

Your verdict is "not guilty" if you've accepted Jesus Christ. Walk out of the prison doors that Satan has put you behind. Jesus has set you free.

Daily Notes: _____

_____

_____

_____

_____

_____

_____

_____

_____

_____

_____

JIMINY

January 18

Jiminy Cricket: character from Disney's movies, Pinocchio.

> **John 16:13** — *Howbeit when he, the spirit of truth, is come, he will guide you into all truth: for he shall not speak of himself; but whatsoever he shall hear, that shall he speak: and he will shew you things to come.*

Testimony

Jiminy is a cricket whose famous line is "let your conscience be your guide!" Who's in control of your conscience? If you've accepted Jesus, you have received the Holy Spirit. The Holy Spirit is your guide. Every day the Holy Spirit will speak to you in different ways to let you know if what you're doing is lining up with the Word of God.

Mission

Who are you letting be your guide? If it's not Jesus, then change drivers.

Daily Notes: _____

_____

_____

_____

_____

_____

_____

_____

_____

_____

JORDAN

January 19

Jordan: river in ancient Palestine.

Matthew 3:16 — *And Jesus, when he was baptized, went up straightway out of the water: and, lo, the heavens were opened unto Him, and He saw the Spirit of God descending like a dove, and lighting upon him:*

Testimony

Jesus didn't need to be baptized because he never sinned. He is perfect. Everything Jesus did, He did for us. We should follow His example. God was pleased with Jesus when He was baptized. Baptism is an outward confession of an inward change. Jesus wants us to follow His example.

Mission

If you've never been baptized, then speak to your pastor, and most importantly, Jesus, about being baptized. Show the world that you choose to follow Jesus.

Daily Notes: _____

_____

_____

_____

_____

_____

_____

_____

_____

JOHN

John: the apostle John, believed to be the author of the fourth Gospel, three Epistles, and the book of Revelation.

> **John 3:16 —** *For God so loved the world that he gave his only begotten Son, that whosoever believeth in him should not perish, but have everlasting life.*

Testimony

Jesus loves us that much. He gave it all. He held nothing back. He did it all for you. All you have to do is believe it.

Mission

Believe.

Daily Notes: _____

_____

_____

_____

_____

_____

_____

_____

_____

_____

_____

_____

_____

_____

JAMES

January 21

James: The son of Zebedee and Salome; an elder brother of John the apostle. He was one of the twelve. He was by trade a fisherman, in partnership with Peter.

> **James 1:17** — *every good gift and every perfect gift is from above, and cometh down from the Father of lights, with whom is no variableness, neither shadow of turning.*

Testimony

Is there a reason the word testimony has the word test in it? I don't think so. During our trials, we have to remember that God is always good and perfect. He never tempts us with evil. When we are tempted or in a trial, we have to remember who is always good and perfect. Give your situation to the Lord and let the One who is good and perfect, make good and perfect come out of it.

As I was typing this, my dog kept looking at me. She started barking and whining. I looked back at her and said, "Jump! Come on! All you have to do is jump and you will be on my lap." Isn't God looking at us and saying the same thing. All you have to do is trust me. I have already provided the good and perfect way for you. Just jump.

Mission

When things are not in your favor or going your way, remember who is for you, and who is good and perfect. Cling to Jesus. Only goodness will follow.

Daily Notes: _____

_____

_____

_____

JUMBLED

January 22

Jumbled: to mix in a confused mass; put or throw together without order:

>**1 Corinthians 14:33** — *God is not the author of confusion, but of peace, as in all churches of the saints.*

Testimony

We all have times in our lives where we are just confused. In those moments do we ever stop and evaluate why? God is not the author of confusion, satan is. God's way is a straight and narrow path to the truth. When I experience confusion in my life, it's because I've taken my mind off of Jesus and put it on my circumstances.

Mission

When you're confused, go to the Word. The Word will lead you to the clear-cut answers you're looking for. There is no confusion in Christ.

Daily Notes: _____

_____

_____

_____

_____

_____

_____

_____

_____

JOKER

January 23

Joker: a person who jokes.

> **Exodus 14:25** — *And took off their chariot wheels, that they drave them heavily: so that the Egyptians said, Let us flee from the face of Israel; for the Lord fighteth for them against the Egyptians.*

Testimony

Could you imagine driving a vehicle and all of the sudden the wheels are thrown off? The Egyptians, chasing after the children of Israel, experienced that in their chariots. Sometimes we view the Lord as being so serious all the time; but this image gives us the expression that Jesus is capable of joking around. The Lord has a sense of humor and He knows ours.

Mission

There is a time to be serious and a time you can joke around. In those funny moments, soak it up, laugh, and enjoy the life God has given you. In those moments look for the hand of the Lord making everything work perfect for you in the perfect way.

Daily Notes: _____

_____

_____

_____

_____

_____

_____

_____

JIG

January 24

Jig: to dance (a jig or any lively dance).

> **2 Samuel 6:14** — *And David danced before the Lord with all his might; and David was grided with a linen ephod.*

Testimony

Have you ever felt so overwhelmed with God's greatness and blessings for you that you did something out of the ordinary? David danced! He leaped before the Lord. He showed he was grateful. How do you show the Lord you're grateful? How do you show others that you're excited about what God's done for you?

Mission

Whether it's dancing, singing, shouting, skipping, leaping, or running, show the Lord you're grateful. It's exciting and fun to serve the Lord! We need to show the lost how great Jesus is!

Daily Notes: _____

_____

_____

_____

_____

_____

_____

_____

_____

_____

_____

JONATHAN

January 25

Jonathan: a son of Saul and friend of David.

> **1 Samuel 18:1** — *And it came to pass, when he had made an end of speaking unto Saul, that the soul of Jonathan was knit with the soul of David, and Jonathan loved him as his own soul.*

Testimony

Jonathan had given up his rightful throne to David. God wanted David to be king. Jonathan knew that and was obedient to God's will. This would have been hard for anybody, but Jonathan had a brotherly love for David. Their souls were knit together. This type of feeling of respect and genuine caring was only possible through the Lord. This shows us that Jesus can change our feelings to match His will.

Jonathan did everything with gladness because he served the Lord. He was a humble man and a great example of humility that Jesus calls us all to be.

Mission

Make sure your feelings are matching up with God's Word. Ask Jesus to change your feelings about situations in your life to match His will for you. Be humble.

Daily Notes: _____

_____

_____

_____

_____

_____

JESSE

January 26

Jesse: the father of David. A male given name: from a Hebrew word meaning "God exists."

> **1 Samuel 17:17 —** *And Jesse said unto David his son, Take now for thy brethren an ephah of this parched corn, and these ten loaves, and run to camp to thy brethren;*

Testimony

Sometimes we go about our day like "What's the point in this?" Then God calls us. God called David to do what all the other men were afraid to do. David's role in the battle was to deliver the food like his father told him to, but his Heavenly Father had other plans. David killed the giant Goliath with the skills God equipped him with. He didn't need a sword, shield, or armor. All he needed was the willingness to be obedient and trust that his Heavenly Father would deliver him.

Mission

When facing a battle, know that no Goliath is too big for your Heavenly Father. All you have to do is trust that God will equip you and deliver you from evil.

Daily Notes: _____

_____

_____

_____

_____

_____

_____

JUDAH

January 27

Judah: one of the twelve tribes of Israel.

> **2 Samuel 2:4** — *And the men of Judah came, and there they anointed David king over the house of Judah. And they told David, saying, that the men of Jabesh-gilead were they that buried Saul.*

Testimony

In the books of Samuel we see the transformation of David. We see the plans the world had for David and then we see the plans God had for David. David submitted to Gods' plan—not the world's or the opinion of others. He followed what God told him to do.

Mission

Don't limit yourself. When you limit yourself, you limit God. God's plans are greater than any you have for yourself. Tune into what God's saying and not what the world's shouting.

Daily Notes: _____

_____

_____

_____

_____

_____

_____

_____

_____

JABESH-GILEAD

January 28

Jabesh-gilead: took down the bodies of Saul and of his three sons from the walls of Beth-shan, and after burning them, buried the bones under a tree near the city.

> **2 Samuel 2:5 —** *And David sent messengers unto the men of Jabesh-gilead, and said unto them, Blessed be ye of the Lord, that ye have shewed this kindness unto your Lord, even unto Saul, and have buried him.*

Testimony

Because of their kindness, they were blessed. The Lord showed them kindness and truth, and so did David. No random act of kindness goes unnoticed by our Savior. We are called to love and show love to others. We are called to esteem others before ourselves. Be a blessing to others and let the Lord bless you.

Mission

Don't ever get burnt out when showing kindness to others, even when they don't deserve it. Jesus will bless you for your kindness.

Daily Notes: _____

_____

_____

_____

_____

_____

_____

JUMP

January 29

Jump: to rise suddenly or quickly.

> **Matthew 4:9** — *And saith unto him, All these things will I give thee, if thou wilt fall down and worship me.*

Testimony

This was the third temptation of satan towards Jesus. Satan tempted him by telling Him to fall down and acknowledge him as having power. I can imagine Jesus jumping up, doing the exact opposite of falling down to worship as He said, "Get thee hence, Satan: for it is written, Thou shalt worship the Lord thy God, and Him only shalt thou serve." After that response, satan had to flee.

Mission

When satan tries to tempt you, remember Jesus' words and say, "In Jesus name, leave!" Satan has to flee!

Daily Notes: _____

_____

_____

_____

_____

_____

_____

_____

_____

_____

JAY

January 30

Jay: any of several noisy, vivacious birds of the crow family.

> **Matthew 6:26** — *behold the fowls of the air: for they sow not, neither do they reap, nor gather into barns; yet your heavenly Father feedeth them. Are ye not much better than they?*

Testimony

In dark situations and hard times it's easy to feel sorry for yourself. In fact in your situation you may have every right to feel sorry for yourself. But does Jesus want us to feel this way? No. Jesus said, "I take care of the birds. How much more will I take care of you?"

Mission

When you're feeling sorry for yourself, remember God's promises. Remember how He is working everything out for your good and His glory. He loves you.

Daily Notes: _____

_____

_____

_____

_____

_____

_____

_____

_____

_____

JANUARY

January 31

Reflection of the month of January:

Proverbs 3:12 — *For whom the LORD loveth he correcteth; even as a father the son in whom he delighteth.*

Testimony

I hope at the end of this month you can say God's correcting you and showing you His love. Sometimes correction hurts; but if God's correcting us, it's because He loves us and is transforming us to look more like Him and less like the world.

Mission

Go back and read your favorite devotions from this past month. Reflect on what you have learned. Take notes on how God is changing your life and correcting your paths. Don't forget what God's done for you and what He is continuing to do. Write down the correction that has taken place this month so you don't forget them. Thank the Lord for the correction that has taken place to make you look more like Him.

Daily Notes: _____

_____

_____

_____

_____

_____

_____

_____

_____

FEAR

Fear: is an unpleasant emotion caused by the belief that something is dangerous. It is the feeling of an alarm, tension, horror or terror.

2 Timothy 1:7 — *For God hath not given us a spirit of fear; but of power, and love, and of a sound mind.*

Testimony

I experience fear often when I'm alone. A sermon I heard changed my perspective. It said, "Fear does not belong to us. Who told you to fear? It is not a spirit from the Lord! That gut wrenching feeling is from satan. Satan has to have your permission to allow you to fear."

A little boy in our church told his mother who was experiencing fear as she prepared to sing, "Mom JESUS doesn't make you feel like you have to throw up." How funny, but so true.

My husband said it best, "Fear does not belong to you!"

Mission

Fear belongs to satan. He creates it. When feelings of fear arise, remember who it belongs and give it back. Believe that JESUS doesn't want you to fear, but to trust Him. Don't let fear stop you from experiencing all JESUS has for you.

Daily Notes: _____

_____

_____

_____

_____

_____

_____

FREE

Free: Not imprisoned or confined. Not controlled by obligation or the will of another. Felt free to go; without restraint. To relieve of a burden, obligation, or restraint. To remove obstructions or entanglements.

> **Exodus 14:21** — *And Moses stretched out his hand over the sea; and the Lord caused the sea to go back by a strong east wind all that night, and made the sea dry land, and the waters were divided.*

Testimony

You plead my cause. You right my wrong. You break my chains. You overcome. You gave your life to give me mine. You say that I am free. How can it be? These are the lyrics from Lauren Daigle's song "How Can It Be." Jesus sets us free. It's only in Him that we truly are free. Moses didn't look at the sea and say, "that's it, we're stuck." He knew he was free in Jesus. The waters were divided for Moses and the children of Israel and they walked through it freely.

Mission

When you find yourself at a dead end, don't look back. Instead look up to Jesus and let him divided your troubled waters. Moses stretched out his hand. Stretch out your heart to Jesus.

Daily Notes: _____

_____

_____

_____

_____

_____

FACT

February 3

Fact: Reality of a situation.

> **John 8:32** — *And ye shall know the truth, and the truth shall make you free.*

Testimony
Freedom comes when we surrender. We discover truth when we give ourselves completely to our Savior. The truth about our sinful nature becomes a reality the day we pray the prayer of salvation. We recognize we are in need of a Savior. When we accept the truth, Jesus sets us free forever from the bondage of sin.

Mission
Jesus is truth. Jesus is the only way to set you free. Accept reality.

Daily Notes: _____

_____

_____

_____

_____

_____

_____

_____

_____

_____

_____

FALL

Fall: to become less or lower; become of a lower level, degree, amount, quality, value, number, etc.; decline:

> **Daniel 3:5** — *That at what time ye hear the sound of the cornet, flute, harp, sackbut, psaltery, dulcimer, and all kinds of musick, ye fall down and worship the golden image that Nebuchadnezzar the king hath set up.*

Testimony

Three men did not fall down and worship the golden images. When the entire nation bowed down, they stood their ground and wouldn't bow — three out of the entire nation. Don't fall in your circumstances. We are talking about three men verses a nation. However, three men with Jesus is not a problem.

I was at church one day and fell down and prayed at the altar. A girl in our church stood up and said, "as soon as your knees hit the ground," Jesus said, "It's taken care of!" Now every time I go to my knees to pray I think of Jesus saying "It's taken care of!"

Mission

Don't fall down and worship the things of this world or follow the crowd. Know that the only One worthy for us to bow down and worship is our Savior. When you do bow down to pray, know that "It's taken care of."

Daily Notes: _____

_____

_____

_____

_____

FELL

February 5

Fell: to knock, strike, shoot, or cut down; cause to fall

Daniel 3:7 — *Therefore at that time, when all the people heard the sound of the cornet, flute, harp, sackbut, psaltery, and all kinds of musick, all the people, the nations, and the languages, fell down and worshipped the golden image Nebuchadnezzar the king had set up.*

Testimony

What if your obedience to the Lord meant going against the king who ruled over you — the king who decided whether you lived or died. How bold would you be? Would you be obedient if it meant death? Shadrach, Meshach, and Abed-nego were that bold.

Mission

Get out of your comfort zone. Get into God's will for your life. Jesus is with us in and out of our comfort zone. But if we want to receive all Jesus has for us, it might just require us to take a step out of our comfort zone. Do it!

Daily Notes: _____

_____

_____

_____

_____

_____

_____

_____

_____

FIERY

February 6

Fiery: intensely hot

> **Daniel 3:17** — *If it be so, our God whom we serve is able to deliver us from the burning fiery furnace, and he will deliver us out of thine hand, O king.*

Testimony

Shadrach, Meshach, and Abed-nego were bold. Where did their boldness come from? It came from serving a living God! Their answer throughout this chapter in Daniel, towards the king, shows their confidence in their living Savior. At one point they said to the king, "We are not careful to answer thee in this matter!" They had so much trust in their Savior! They knew God's will would be done. They didn't care whether they lived or died because they knew God's will is perfect. His way is best and ultimately His will shall be done.

Mission

Don't compromise situations when it comes to the Lord. Stand up for the Word of God no matter what. Jesus will bless you for it regardless of how fiery the furnace is.

Daily Notes: _____

_____

_____

_____

_____

_____

_____

_____

FURNACE

Furnace: an enclosed chamber in which heat is produced to generate steam, destroy, refuse, smelt or refine.

> **Daniel 3:25** — *He answered and said, Lo, I see four men loose, walking in the midst of the fire, and they have no hurt; and the form of the fourth is like the Son of God.*

Testimony

Nebuchadnezzar the king threw the three men into the fire, but later he saw four men in the fire. Jesus is with us in the fire. He saves us and protects us. He protected the three men. Nebuchadnezzar called for the three men to come out of the fire. He didn't want anything to do with the fourth man. When they walked out of the furnace, they didn't even smell like smoke. When we give our trials to Jesus, we too will be brand new. Jesus doesn't leave any cracks or left over smudges from our past to cover up His glory. After this, Nebuchadnezzar passed a decree that everyone had to worship Shadrach, Meshach, and Abed-nego's God. The three men that went against a nation with Jesus, ended up changing the nation!

Mission

Everything about a fire is intimating, however, you can face anything in your life if you keep your eyes focused on Jesus. He is with you in the fire. Hold on! He'll bring you through your trials and you will shine.

Daily Notes: _____

_____

_____

_____

_____

FEARLESS

Fearless: without fear; bold or brave; intrepid.

> **Acts 14:3** — *Long time therefore abode they speaking boldly in the Lord, which gave testimony unto the word of his grace, and granted signs and wonders to be done by their hands.*

Testimony

Paul spoke boldly about the Lord to the people. As a result of doing so, Paul was stoned and thrown out of the city. What does Paul do about it? After being stoned and left for dead, Paul got up and went back into the city to speak boldly about the Lord again.

Mission

Be bold for the Lord. Look at the examples the disciples left for us to follow. In what ways is the Lord asking you to be bold in your life right now?

Daily Notes: _____

_____

_____

_____

_____

_____

_____

_____

_____

_____

FREEDOM

Freedom: the state of being free or at liberty rather than in confinement or under physical restraint.

Proverbs 18:21 — *Death and life are in the power of the tongue: and they that love it shall eat the fruit thereof.*

Testimony

We have power in our spoken words. Sometimes we can be our harshest critics! We need to wake up every day speaking the truth over ourselves, instead of focusing on our imperfections. The truth is, we are blessed and made in the image of Christ. A famous preacher, Steven Furtick, mentioned in a sermon "when we doubt the product, we doubt the manufacture. Christ is the manufacture and we are His products."

Mission

Speak life. Freedom comes from speaking life into your own life, the lives of others, and your circumstances. Jesus died to set you free.

Daily Notes: _____

_____

_____

_____

_____

_____

_____

_____

FIRST

February 10

First: being before all others with respect to time, order, rank, importance, etc., used as the ordinal number of one:

> **Exodus 13:21** — *And the Lord went before them by day in a pillar of a cloud, to lead them the way; and by night in a pillar of fire, to give them light; to go by day and night:*

Testimony

Jesus gave the Israelites what they needed when they needed it; but they had to put Him first. When they took their eyes off Jesus and focused on themselves and their circumstances, they got lost. Jesus has never been lost. You won't be lost either if you keep your eyes focused on the Lord and let Him lead you. He gave them what they needed: a cloud in the day. A cloud during a hot summer day provides us with shelter and shade. A fire at night provides us with warmth and light to see. The Lord always knows what He's doing and the perfect way to lead us.

Mission

If you want order in your life, then put your life in order. Jesus has to be first.

Daily Notes: _____

_____

_____

_____

_____

_____

_____

_____

FREAK

Jesus Freak: a Christian with an intense enthusiasm for Jesus Christ and His teachings.

> **Galatians 2:20** — *I am crucified with Christ: nevertheless I live; yet not I, but Christ liveth in me: and the life which I now live in the flesh I live by the faith of the Son of God, who loved me, and gave himself for me.*

Testimony

First of all, Jesus Freak is an actual term in the dictionary. Praise the Lord! This verse shows us what a Jesus Freak looks like. Paul was a Jesus Freak. Being a Jesus Freak gets to the point where you no longer acknowledge your desires, morals, or virtues, but you acknowledge your dependency on Jesus for strength and all necessities.

When you add chocolate to your milk, you get chocolate milk. There is no way to separate the chocolate from the milk after you add the chocolate and stir it up. This is what we should look like with Jesus.

Once we accept Him, people should look at us and see Him. There should be no separation between Him and us. So as my pastor, Todd King, would say, "Keep it stirred up! Keep Jesus stirred up inside of you."

Mission

John 3:30 — *He must increase, but I must decrease.*

Daily Notes: _____

_____

_____

_____

FOOLISH

February 12

Foolish: resulting from or showing a lack of sense; ill-considered; unwise:

> **Matthew 7:26** — *And every one that heareth these sayings of mine, and doeth them not, shall be likened unto a foolish man, which built his house upon the sand.*

Testimony

Jesus is saying that 'hearing' without 'doing' lays a wrong foundation. It's not the failure of labor, but the failure of a proper foundation that hinders our walk with the Lord. We have to make a heart connection. You might know in your head the right things to do, but without the heart behind it, the foundation won't stand. Who knows our heart's truest desires? Jesus created us and knows our heart's desires. Jesus gave us His Word to prepare and build the proper foundation. You can find proper instructions, everything you want to know from the Word of God. Will you build your house on rock or sand? Will you settle for head knowledge and not invest your heart?

Mission

Jesus is our rock and we want our house built upon Him. Don't build upon anything in your life other than Jesus. He is the only One that will stand. Make a heart connection!

Daily Notes: _____

_____

_____

_____

_____

FORWARD

Forward: toward or at a place, point, or time in advance; onward;

Philippians 3:13 — *Brethren, I count not myself to have apprehended: but this one thing I do, forgetting those things which are behind, and reaching forth unto those things which are before,*

Testimony

In order to move forward, you can't look back. Yes, we're going to fall in life sometimes, but just make sure you fall forward. We don't want to go back. Remembering where you came from and what God has delivered you from is one thing; but staying there and letting guilt keep you from experiencing your future with God is not OK anymore. Jesus wants you to move forward. Every day you're either growing or dying.

Mission

Grow and go forward with the Lord. Everyday get closer.

Daily Notes: _____

_____

_____

_____

_____

_____

_____

_____

_____

_____

FIRM

Firm: securely fixed in place.

> **2 Samuel 6:6** — *And when they came to Nachon's threshing floor, Uzzah put forth his hand to the ark of God, and took hold of it; for the oxen shook it.*

Testimony

The ark was being moved. The Lord said for no human hand to touch it. It became unsteady so Uzzah touched it to stabilize it. He died. Doing God's work is a serious business. Look at the consequences for disobeying what God commanded. In our life going against God's Word can mean a life full of pain and sometimes, worse. If we don't accept Jesus as our Savior, it could mean spending an eternity in hell. There are consequences for sin and disobeying God. Don't gamble. The odds are clear. Sin equals death and Jesus is life.

Mission

Don't take serving Jesus lightly. He didn't take giving His life for you lightly.

Daily Notes: _____

_____

_____

_____

_____

_____

_____

_____

_____

FOREVER

Forever: without ever ending; eternally:

Psalm 23:1-6 — *The Lord is my shepherd; I shall not want. He maketh me to lie down in green pastures: he leadeth me beside the still waters. He restoreth my soul: he leadeth me in the paths of righteousness for his name's sake. Yea, though I walk through the valley of the shadow of death, I will fear no evil: for thou art with me; thy rod and thy staff they comfort me. Thou preparest a table before me in the presence of mine enemies: thou anointest my head with oil; my cup runneth over. Surely goodness and mercy shall follow me all the days of my life: and I will dwell in the house of the Lord forever.*

Testimony

Jesus is our protector and provider in life now and forever. I was watching a television commercial for e-Harmony®. The commercial said, "Do you want it fast or forever?" Jesus spoke to me about that commercial and showed me that is how He is working out the details of our lives. We want it now. We want it fast. But Jesus is working out our forever. When Jesus says or does something, it's forever. He is our forever.

Mission

Make Jesus your forever, and make your forever home with Him too. He's waiting.

Daily Notes: _____

_____

_____

_____

FORM

Form: the shape of a thing or person.

> **2 Corinthians 3:18** — *While we look not at the things which are seen, but at the things which are not seen: for the things which are seen are temporal; but the things which are not seen are eternal.*

Testimony

A man in our church was teaching and he put his hands over a flashlight. He said, "no matter what, some light will shine through the cracks of your hands." That's how the light of the Lord is coming out in us. It wants to come out. We might not demonstrate it all the time, but it's there all the time. We need to get to the point that we're not covering it up at all, but instead waving it around in the air making sure it's seen.

Mission

Transform into the image of Christ. Let your light be seen. Just a little bit of light can light up a room full of darkness. You can see a light from far away. Be that transforming light.

Daily Notes: _____

_____

_____

_____

_____

_____

_____

FIND

Find: to locate or recover

Luke 11:9 — *And I say unto you, Ask, and it shall be given you; seek, and ye shall find; knock and it shall be opened unto you.*

Testimony

This is the way the Bible says to model prayer. We need to have confidence in our prayers. Faith says to thank Jesus for something that hasn't been accomplished yet, and acknowledge that God is in control and He will do it. Every man has been dealt a measure of faith. You weren't exempt when God created you. You have the faith to believe that Jesus is here, will answer your prayers, and hears every word you say. Jesus isn't lost. He doesn't need to be found, but you need to make sure you find Him.

Mission

Find Jesus. He isn't lost. If you haven't found Him, you are.

Daily Notes: _____

_____

_____

_____

_____

_____

_____

_____

_____

_____

FISHERMEN

February 18

Fishermen: a person who fishes, whether for profit or pleasure.

John 21:6 — *And he said unto them, Cast the net on the right side of the ship, and ye shall find. They cast therefore, and now they were not able to draw it for the multitude of fishes.*

Testimony

The disciples had been fishing all night. They came back empty handed and Jesus was standing on the shore. He told them to cast their nets to the right side. They then had so many fish that they were not able to draw the net out of the water. Isn't that just like Jesus when we ask Him for something. He always gives us so much more than we expected. He is that good. He not only gave them what they needed, He gave them so much more.

Mission

When you pray, trust Jesus. Know that He is good and He is working it out for your good. He will not only give you what you need, He will go beyond that. Let His blessings flow and trust Him in every area of your life.

Daily Notes: _____

_____

_____

_____

_____

_____

_____

FASCINATE

February 19

Fascinate: to attract and hold attentively by a unique power, personal charm, unusual nature, or some other special quality.

John 21:7 — *Therefore that disciple whom Jesus loved saith unto Peter, It is the Lord. Now when Simon Peter heard that it was the Lord, he girt his fishers coat unto him, (for he was naked,) and did cast himself into the sea.*

Testimony

Jesus was standing on the shore. Once the disciples figured out it was the Lord, Peter jumped out of the boat, threw himself into the sea, and walked towards His Jesus. The other disciples stayed in a little ship. Which disciple are you? Are you so excited that you're jumping? Or are you waiting it out while saying, "Well, it's just the Lord. Let's get this boat ready and take our good sweet time. He will still be there when we make it."

Mission

Be the one jumping for the Lord! Peter was fascinated with His Jesus. Be fascinated with Jesus!

Daily Notes: _____

_____

_____

_____

_____

_____

_____

_____

FIRE

Fire: a burning mass of material, as on a hearth or in a furnace.

Exodus 3:2 — *And the angle of the Lord appeared unto him in a flame of fire out of the midst of a bush: and he looked, and behold, the bush burned with fire, and the bush was not consumed.*

Testimony

This was a miracle. A fire will spread and burn up anything it touches. However, the bush was not consumed. We too, as God's people, will not be consumed in a fiery trial, if we keep our eyes fixed on Jesus, the author and finisher of our faith. He gives peace in all situations. We will stand alive like the bush after it had been consumed by fire.

Mission

Follow Christ. Do not let yourself be consumed by the world, but let yourself be transformed by Jesus.

Daily Notes: _____

_____

_____

_____

_____

_____

_____

_____

_____

FOLLOW

February 21

Follow: to go or come after; move behind in the same direction:

Acts 28:4 — *And when the barbarians saw the venomous beast hang on his hand, they said among themselves, no doubt this man is a murderer, whom, though he hath escaped the sea, yet vengeance suffereth not to live.*

Testimony

Paul had just suffered a massive shipwreck. Paul washed up on the shore of the island Melita and was greeted by a barbarous people. They had built a fire and out of it came a viper. It fastened on to Paul's hand. He simply shook it off back into the fire and felt no harm.

Jesus knew what it would take for these barbarians to follow Him. Jesus knew what these people understood. They understood that the viper was poisonous and anyone bitten by it should have died. Jesus knows us and knows what it's going to take for us to follow Him. Each one of us comes to Him in a special unique way.

Mission

Have you ever been around someone that just "gets you"? You have. Jesus "gets you" and knows you inside and out. Let Him speak to you in that special way.

Daily Notes: _____

_____

_____

_____

_____

_____

FRUITS

February 22

Fruits: anything produced or accruing; product, result, or effect; return or profit:

> **Proverbs 3:9** — *Honor the Lord with thy substance, and with the frustrates of all thine increase:*

Testimony

Everything we have has been given to us from the Lord. Therefore we should honor Him with all that we have from Him — our time, money, resources, and our heart. The result of putting Jesus first in all we have and do, is like having a barn that would be filled and wine presses that would burst with new wine. We won't be able to contain all the goodness that comes from giving Jesus our first fruits!

Mission

Don't give Jesus the last part of your day, time, and finances. Give Jesus the best part of it all and make it first. Then watch the fruit produce.

Daily Notes: _____

_____

_____

_____

_____

_____

_____

_____

FAMILY

February 23

Family: a group of persons who form a household under one head, including parents, children, and servants.

> **Ecclesiastes 4:12** — *And if one prevail against him, two shall withstand him; and a threefold chord is not quickly broken.*

Testimony

The household is under one head according to the definition of family. Make that leader of the family Jesus Christ. A threefold chord is not quickly broken. Jesus needs to be first and in charge of your family. A family that prays together stays together. Jesus makes that perfect threefold chord, but He has to be first. Put Jesus in all your family decisions, so your family is in the will of God.

Mission

Evaluate who is in charge of your household. If it's not Jesus, then prioritize. He's the only way to truth, and life.

Daily Notes: _____

_____

_____

_____

_____

_____

_____

_____

_____

FIELDS

February 24

Fields: an expanse of open or cleared ground, especially a piece of land suitable or used for pasture or tillage.

> **Ruth 2:2** — *And Ruth the Moabitess said unto Naomi, Let me now go to the field, and glean ears of corn after him in whose sight I shall find grace. And she said unto her, Go, my daughter.*

Testimony

Ruth "happened" to be in the field that Boaz was in. This is the sign of how wonderful and in control of our lives, Jesus is. The plan was for Ruth to find grace in Boaz's sight. She spoke life to her mother-in-law in verse two. Once she sees that she is indeed gaining the grace of Boaz, she questions him.

Isn't this just like us? We can speak life and trust in Jesus, but once our prayers are answered, we question Him. We serve a gracious God who continuously confirms His will for us. Boaz confirms to Ruth why he has recognized her, and he gives credit to the Lord in whom she has recently come to trust.

Mission

Trust builds a relationship. Ruth found her trust in Jesus in a field. Trust Jesus in the fields of your life.

Daily Notes: _____

_____

_____

_____

_____

_____

FAST

Fast: moving or able to move, operate, function, or take effect quickly; quick; swift; rapid:

> **Ruth 3:18** — *Then said she, Sit still, my daughter, until thou know how the matter will fall: for the man will not be in rest, until he have finished the thing this day.*

Testimony

Sometimes we want to move and do everything so fast. We live in a fast paced, ever-changing environment. Sometimes in serving the Lord, we need to act quickly. Other times, like in this verse, we need to wait. The advice Naomi gives Ruth is to sit still. When waiting to hear from the Lord, don't have anxiety in your hearts, but instead trust that the Lord is in control working things out for our good.

Sometimes our obedience to the Lord requires us to wait.

Mission

The Lord knows how our lives will play out. When things are out of our control, we need to sit still, not move fast, and wait for the Lord to work things out. Wait on the Lord.

Daily Notes: _____

_____

_____

_____

_____

_____

_____

FRIEND

February 26

Friend: a person attached to another by feelings of affection or personal regard.

> **Genesis 25:31 —** *And Jacob said, Sell me this day thy birthright.*

Testimony

A famous preacher once said that when Esau sold his birthright to Jacob, all he needed was one good friend to say, "Esau, what are you doing? You're about to sell your birthright for a bowl of soup!" One good friend can make a difference in your life and influence the decisions you make.

Mission

Be that one good friend towards someone who leads him or her into the will of God. Don't be a friend that leads them astray.

Daily Notes: _____

_____

_____

_____

_____

_____

_____

_____

_____

_____

_____

FARTHER

February 27

Farther: at or to a greater degree or extent.

> **Judges 6:12** — *And the angel of the Lord appeared unto him, and said unto him, The Lord is with thee, thou mighty man of valour.*

Testimony

When the angel of the Lord appeared unto Gideon, he didn't tell Gideon God's entire plan for him. If the angel of the Lord had told him, "You will defeat a huge army with 300 men," Gideon might not have believed it was from God. Instead, the Lord revealed His plan, one step at a time. With each step, Gideon went further and further with the Lord.

Mission

You might feel like you're in a baby step moment of your life right now. Know that God will take you further. He is building you up. Nothing is insignificant with Jesus. Start today and allow God to take you further and further in Him, showing you step by step.

Daily Notes: _____

_____

_____

_____

_____

_____

_____

_____

FURTHER

February 28

Further: at or to a more advanced point; to a greater extent:

Judges 8:23 — *And Gideon said unto them, I will not rule over you, neither shall my son rule over you: the Lord shall rule over you.*

Testimony

God is good. He takes us further than we ever expect. God took Gideon from hiding, to a leader of an army, then to be ruler over Israel. Gideon took it a step further. When the children of Israel said, "We want you to rule," Gideon furthered his authority and gave all authority and credit to our Lord. As a result, during Gideon's entire life, the country was at peace.

Mission

Don't give yourself credit; Jesus created you. Offer up praise to the Lord for each step of your life. As a result, you will have peace.

Daily Notes: _____

_____

_____

_____

_____

_____

_____

_____

_____

_____

FEBRUARY

Reflection of the month of February:

Judges 8:34 — *And the children of Israel remembered not the Lord their God, who had delivered them out of the hands of all their enemies on every side:*

John 15:5 — *For without me ye can do nothing.*

Testimony

God had transformed and provided for the children of Israel time and time again. They remembered Him not. Don't fail to remember who is your everything and gave you everything — including His life. Don't forget that without Him, you can do nothing; but with Him, you can do all things.

Mission

Remember your transformation. Remember what your old man looked like before God put His spirit inside of you and created you as a new man in His perfect, Holy image. Reflect on your transformation. Go back and read your favorite devotionals from February. Thank God for the powerful, wonderful, transformation He has done in you.

Daily Notes: _____

_____

_____

_____

_____

_____

_____

MY

March 1

My: a form of the possessive case of I used as an attributive adjective

> **Psalms 19:14** — *Let the words of my mouth, and the meditation of my heart, be acceptable in thy sight, O LORD, my strength, and my redeemer.*

Testimony

When you use the word "my" when talking about yourself, you're taking ownership. If we have accepted Christ, we need to take how we represent Him seriously. In Psalms 19:14, David is accountable for the words out of his mouth, making sure his heart and his words are acceptable to the Lord. The Lord is everything to us. If we have nothing but trust in the Lord, we have everything. He is our everything. We need to show the world that.

Mission

Be like David. Make sure your mouth and heart line up with the Word of Christ and is acceptable in His sight.

Daily Notes: _____

_____

_____

_____

_____

_____

_____

_____

_____

MARRIED

March 2

Married: of or relating to marriage or married persons; connubial; conjugal:

Ephesians 5:33 — *Nevertheless let every one of you in particular so love his wife even as himself; and the wife [see] that she reverence [her] husband.*

Testimony

The end of this chapter gives us the instructions for marriage summed up in a phrase I like to call "JOY" —

1. Jesus 2. Others 3. Yourself

We are to prefer our husbands or wives better than ourselves and above all, put Jesus first. In everything you do, display the love of Christ. Never make divorce an option. When you married your spouse, you made a promise to the Lord. Allow Jesus to lead your marriage into His perfect plan for it. If you're not married yet, wait upon the Lord to send you the perfect spouse. He has the perfect one picked out just for you.

Marriage

The two become one flesh. Make sure your marriage is focused on moving towards Christ. Pray for God to take hold of your hearts, desires, and lead you and your husband [or wife] into His plan for your marriage.

Daily Notes: _____

_____

_____

_____

_____

MAKER

March 3

Maker: a manufacturer

> **Isaiah 54:5** — *For your Maker is your husband, the LORD of hosts is his name; and the Redeemer the Holy One of Israel; The God of the whole earth shall he be called.*

Testimony

This chapter in Isaiah declares who your true Maker is. The verse focuses on the Gentiles who are depicted as a barren and desolate woman that break forth into songs of praise, despite their barren situation. This gives us an image of how good God is, showing His everlasting kindness towards us. Jesus is the Maker and Redeemer of all men — the same One who is the Holy One. Even in a dark situation, we can praise God. Watch the pouting turn into praising.

Mission

Get your eyes off your circumstances and on your Maker.

Daily Notes: _____

_____

_____

_____

_____

_____

_____

_____

_____

MEGIDDO

March 4

Megiddo: an ancient city in N Israel, on the plain of Esdraelon: site of many battles; often identified with the Biblical Armageddon.

> **Judges 5:19** — *The kings came and fought, then fought the kings of Canaan in Taanach by the waters of Megiddo; they took no gain of money.*

Testimony

Megiddo was a city that was all about location. They had walls built and a water supply, yet a lot of people died in Megiddo. They didn't utilize their resources. They had to keep changing methods until they found one that worked. How often before we came to Christ did we utilize other resources — looking to Him as a last resort?

In Megiddo they constructed a huge tunnel they had to walk through to get water. Jesus is our tunnel. We have to run things through Him to get our forever, unquenchable, living water.

Mission

Your resources could run out. Make sure your main resource is Jesus, because He never runs dry.

Daily Notes: _____

_____

_____

_____

_____

_____

_____

MEMORY

March 5

Memory: the mental capacity or faculty of retaining and reviving facts.

Isaiah 43:18 — *Remember ye not the former things, neither consider the things of old.*

Testimony

It's good to remember what Jesus has brought you from, but it's not good to stay in a place where you have already been delivered. Thank Jesus for the past and His healing He has done in your life. Don't stay focused on the person you used to be or the things you used to do. You were made to transform, not conform. Don't live in the past or look back too long. Thank Jesus for it and move on.

Mission

Don't focus on the old you; focus on the new you — created in the perfect imagine of Christ. Jesus makes all things new, including you.

Daily Notes: _____

_____

_____

_____

_____

_____

_____

_____

_____

MEAT

March 6

Meat: the flesh of animals as used for food.

> **Matthew 6:25** — *Therefore I say unto you, Take no thought for your life, what ye shall eat, or what ye shall drink; nor yet for your body, what ye shall put on. Is not the life more than meat, and the body than raiment?*

Testimony

Jesus is saying, "Why worry?" I would say Jesus is being serious when he says, "Take no thought for your life." Jesus is talking about everybody here. No one is exempt. If you're poor, stressed out, whatever your condition might be, you're not excluded. You might be thinking, "Jesus will never understand." Jesus is the only one who will understand, and the only one who will provide. Don't worry about material possessions. You do not want to deprive yourself of the spiritual blessings of God. Look to the spiritual aspect of things verses a material status.

Mission

Don't count on material possessions or a good status to get you by. Focus instead on Jesus and spiritual blessings to carry you through this life into the next. Jesus is saying, "Why worry? I have taken care of it all."

Daily Notes: _____

_____

_____

_____

_____

_____

MEET

Meet: to come upon; come into the presence of; encounter:

> **Romans 10:13** — *For whosoever shall call upon the name of the Lord shall be saved.*

Testimony

Aren't you thankful there was a time when Jesus came to meet you — not that he needed introducing, but that you entered into His presence? A time when you were saved and first accepted Christ? When you called on His name, and He met you right where you were?

Make sure you aren't living your life just occasionally meeting Jesus, but consistently living in His presence.

Mission

Jesus will meet you wherever you're at. Just call upon His name.

Daily Notes: _____

_____

_____

_____

_____

_____

_____

_____

_____

_____

MEANS

Means: to have in mind as ones purpose or intention.

Luke 7:47 — *Wherefore I say unto thee, Her sins, which are many, are forgiven; for she loved much: but to whom little is forgiven, the same loveth little.*

Testimony

The woman had an alabaster box. That was her most precious possession. There was a dinner party at Simon's house, she was not invited. The woman heard where Jesus was, and she went in with her box. She made everyone feel uncomfortable coming in uninvited. She let down her hair crying, and started praising Jesus with tears, and kissing his feet because, she felt unworthy to kiss his face. She was the most blessed yet uninvited guest in the room. Let nothing stop you from getting to Jesus. Make it your means to meet with Jesus no matter how uncomfortable, crazy, or against the world it may seem. Glorify Jesus with everything you have. Give your whole self to Jesus. She left blessed and feeling worthy that day after having met with Jesus.

Mission

What is the means of your life? Make sure it is doing and giving all you can to glorify your Savior.

Daily Notes: _____

_____

_____

_____

_____

_____

MOUNTAIN

Mountain: anything of great quantity or size.

Matthew 17:20 — *And Jesus said unto them, Because of your unbelief: for verily I say unto you, If ye have faith as a grain of mustard seed, ye shall say unto this mountain, Remove hence to yonder place; and it shall remove; and nothing shall be impossible unto you.*

Testimony

My best friend was going through a hard time and Jesus revealed something incredible to her about this verse. She looked up the biggest thing in the world; a mountain. What does Jesus say about a mountain? Jesus says, "By faith tell it to be removed and it shall be removed. Nothing shall be impossible unto you." A mountain is the biggest thing in the world and faith in Jesus can move it. A little bit of Jesus goes all the way.

Mission

The mountains in your life are nothing compared to Jesus. By faith, give Him your mountains and watch them move.

Daily Notes: _____

_____

_____

_____

_____

_____

_____

_____

MAGICIANS

Magicians: an entertainer who is skilled in producing illusion by sleight of hand, deceptive devices, etc.; conjurer.

> **Daniel 4:7** — *Then came in the magicians, the astrologers, the Chaldeans, and the soothsayers: and I told the dream before them, but they did not make known unto me the interpretation thereof.*

Testimony

King Nebuchadnezzar brought in everyone else before he brought in a man of God. Isn't this like us to talk to everyone else? Maybe take the wrong advice from the wrong people before talking to Jesus. Once Nebuchadnezzar talked to Daniel, he knew the truth. He knew what God intended for the dream to mean.

Mission

Just a little talk with Jesus makes it right.

Daily Notes: _____

_____

_____

_____

_____

_____

_____

_____

_____

_____

_____

_____

MEMBER

March 11

Member: a person who belongs

> **1 Corinthians 12:27** — *Now ye are the body of Christ, and members in particular.*

Testimony

Our attitudes should reflect Christ towards one another, and especially those within our church. If you are saved and believe in Jesus, you make up the body of Christ. Satan tries to attack the body of Christ. My sister-in-law told me a story about a woman who had served the Lord a long time in her church.

Another woman who started coming just recently gave her life to the Lord, and she stood up and said, "I feel like no one likes me especially a particular woman she pointed out in the crowd." Now this is not the way to deal with our problems, however, this woman was a young Christian. The woman she pointed out had been serving Christ for a long time, and under the inspiration from the Holy Spirit said, "You have been a burden on my soul. I constantly pray for you. This is a lie from satan." Satan will attack the members of the body of Christ and your relationships within the church. Does satan ever attack your relationships with those who aren't serving the Lord? Beware of the enemy trying to dissemble the members of the body of Christ.

Mission

Pray for the Lord to show you what church He wants you to go to. Also pray for what the Lord wants you to do within the church. Be an active member of the Body of Christ for our Lord.

Daily Notes: _____

_____

MARY

March 12

Mary: also called Virgin Mary. The mother of Jesus.

Matthew 1:20 — *But while he thought on these things, behold the angle of the Lord appeared unto him in a dream, saying, Joseph, thou son of David, fear not to take thee Mary thy wife: for that which is conceived in her is of the Holy Ghost.*

Testimony

Joseph had a dream. It wasn't anything crazy or spectacular, but a dream, and he trusted God. He trusted in the Lord and took already pregnant Mary as his wife. Joseph is a good example of a faithful and trusting man of God.

Mission

No matter what the circumstances, think of Joseph and just trust Jesus with His plan.

Daily Notes: _____

_____

_____

_____

_____

_____

_____

_____

_____

_____

MAGDALENE

March 13

Magdalene: whom Jesus healed of possession by devils.

John 20:16 — *Jesus saith unto her, Mary. She turned herself, and saith unto him, Rabboni; which is to say, Master.*

Testimony

Mary had been possessed, and had suffered mental and physical disabilities. Then she met Jesus! Jesus healed her and she became a devout follower of Christ. She was a leader. She was also the first to see Jesus after he had rolled the stone away. Mary devoted her entire life to serving Christ once she felt the healing touch of Jesus.

Mission

Have you felt the healing touch of Jesus, like Mary? If not, pray to Jesus now. He will heal you. Start right now and devote your entire life to following Christ. You will see Jesus just like Mary did.

Daily Notes: _____

_____

_____

_____

_____

_____

_____

_____

_____

_____

MERRY

March 14

Merry: full of cheerfulness or gaiety; joyous in disposition or spirit:

1 Peter 3:13 — *And who is he that will harm you, if ye be followers of that which is good?*

Testimony

Jesus is asking us a question here. Who will harm you? Know that Jesus has your back. He is good. This scripture is letting us know that we can trust in our loving, good Savior. When we think of a harmful situation, we can get anxious. But Jesus is saying you are followers of that which is good. Be merry. Jesus doesn't want us to be anxious in our spirits when in a harmful situation. We follow a good God in all circumstances, who wants us to be anxious for nothing, but merry in our souls.

Mission

Be merry. You are following a good, gracious God. Only blessings and peace will flow.

Daily Notes: _____

_____

_____

_____

_____

_____

_____

_____

_____

MONEY

Money: any circulating medium of exchange, including coins, paper money, and demand deposits.

> **1 Timothy 6:10** — *For the love of money is the root of all evil: which while some coveted after, they have erred from the faith, and pierced themselves through with many sorrows.*

Testimony

Everything we have is borrowed from Christ. Nothing belongs to us. It all belongs to Him, including money. We tend to think, "it's ours and we have earned it." But, Jesus has equipped us to make that money. Jesus tells us it's better to give than to receive. Don't be hesitant to tithe, or give when needing too.

Tithing is a blessing that Jesus gives us the opportunity to do. Don't become consumed with the love of money.

Mission

Think on Jesus more than you do your finances and bank account. Trust Jesus in that situation. He can take care of your money too.

Daily Notes: _____

_____

_____

_____

_____

_____

_____

_____

MOSES

March 16

Moses: the Hebrew prophet who led the Israelites out of Egypt and delivered the Law during their years of wandering in the wilderness.

> **Exodus 2:3** — *And when she could no longer hide him, she took for him an ark of bulrushes, and daubed it with slime and with pitch, and put the child therein; and she laid it in the flags, by the rivers brink.*

Testimony

The child was Moses. Can you imagine the faith that Moses' mother had in order to be able to do this with her child? This was wisdom received from the Lord. God had big plans for Moses and needed him alive to do His work. God's plan worked. Later Pharaoh's daughter found the infant and called him Moses. She had compassion on him and called for a Hebrew woman to nurse him. It was Moses' mother.

Mission

God's plan is perfect for your life and He has big plans for you. Don't lose sight of that important fact.

Daily Notes: _____

_____

_____

_____

_____

_____

_____

MOAB

Moab: an ancient kingdom east of the Dead Sea, in what is now Jordan.

> **Ruth 1:4** — *And they took them wives of the women of Moab; the name of the one was Orpah, and the name of the other Ruth: and they dwelled there about ten years.*

Testimony

Marriage to a Moabite was not strictly forbidden but severe restrictions were placed on those that entered into the union. However, God had a plan. Naomi was meant to be Ruth's mother-in-law. God knew how the events of the marriage and the relationships of the marriage would play out. God used those relationships to see His plan come together. Ruth was from Moab, but was willing to go and devote herself to Naomi for the rest of her life.

Mission

Where you come from won't deter you from the gorgeous, beautiful plan God has for your life. Let Jesus take you where He wants you to go.

Daily Notes: _____

_____

_____

_____

_____

_____

_____

MATTHEW

Matthew: summoned to be one of the 12 apostles.

> **Matthew 9:9** — *And as Jesus passed forth from thence, he saw a man, named Matthew, sitting at the receipt of custom: and he saith unto him, Follow me. And he arose, and followed him.*

Testimony

Jesus is knocking on your heart's door. Jesus is walking by saying, "Follow me, trust me, just ask, and believe in me." Why are we making it more complicated than that? Matthew didn't. Jesus said, "Follow me." Matthew followed.

Mission

Make it simple. Don't complicate Jesus. Just follow Him.

Daily Notes: _____

_____

_____

_____

_____

_____

_____

_____

_____

_____

_____

_____

MARK

Mark: summoned to be one of the 12 apostles.

> **Mark 2:15** — *And it came to pass, that, as Jesus sat at meat in his house, many publicans and sinners sat also together with Jesus and his disciples: for there were many, and they followed him.*

Testimony

Jesus didn't pick the nicest dressed, best mannered, or one with the best lifestyle to eat with. Jesus ate with the sinners. How else would He have ever won souls?

Mission

Don't be afraid to bump shoulders with the less fortunate people that are different from you. Jesus wants people to hear about him and be saved. Go tell the world.

Daily Notes: _____

_____

_____

_____

_____

_____

_____

_____

_____

_____

MOMENT

March 20

Moment: an indefinitely short period of time; instant:

Exodus 3:4 — *And when the Lord saw that he turned aside to see, God called unto him out of the midst of the burning bush, and said Moses, Moses. And he said, Here am I.*

Testimony

At any moment, God can speak to us in many different ways and call upon us to do great and mighty things. God spoke to Moses in a burning bush and told him what to do. Moses responded and did what the Lord told him to do. How are you responding in your moments when the Lord speaks to you?

Mission

Be like Moses when the Lord calls you. Respond in those moments with, "Here I am."

Daily Notes: _____

_____

_____

_____

_____

_____

_____

_____

_____

_____

_____

MULTITUDES

March 21

Multitudes: a great number of people gathered together; crowd;

Matthew 26:47 — *And while he yet spake, lo, Judas, one of the twelve, came, and with him a great multitude with swords and staves, from the chief priests and elders of the people.*

Testimony

Why send a multitude of people to fetch a man that had never done anything wrong? They had to have known the power in Jesus. He is truly the Son of God. If they didn't know the power, they were about to find out.

While fetching Jesus, one with Him cut off the ear of the soldier. Jesus healed it. The multitudes saw this, yet still took Him to be crucified.

Mission

Don't deny the power of Jesus in your life. Show the world the power in His name.

Daily Notes: _____

_____

_____

_____

_____

_____

_____

_____

MUSTARD SEED

March 22

Mustard Seed: Easy plant to harvest.

Matthew 13:32 — *Which indeed is the least of all seeds: but when it is grown, it is the greatest among herbs, and becometh a tree, so that birds of the air come and lodge in the branches thereof.*

Testimony

The smallest things given to Jesus turns into the biggest. Our faith, church, relationships — when given to Jesus — will grow. Whatever Jesus has you doing, know that it isn't too small to quit. Jesus will bless all you do in His name. The outward appearance of something doesn't always indicate the spiritual growth of a person or situation. Jesus could have you do something that looks so small or insignificant to you, but behind the scenes could be leading someone to salvation.

Mission

Don't quit the small stuff. With Jesus, it turns into big stuff.

Daily Notes: _____

_____

_____

_____

_____

_____

_____

_____

_____

MAN

March 23

Man: the human individual

I Peter 4:2 — *That he no longer should live the rest of his time in the flesh to the lusts of men, but to the will of God.*

Testimony

Who are we to question God's will for our lives? He created us and knows what purpose He has for us. It's good! Lay down your flesh daily and focus on the will of God. The lusts of men will always be tempting if you don't lay your flesh aside.

Mission

Lay down your flesh and lusts, and step into the Will of God.

Daily Notes: _____

_____

_____

_____

_____

_____

_____

_____

_____

_____

_____

_____

_____

MIDIANITES

March 24

Midianites: an Arabian tribe descended from Midian.

> **Judges 6:7** — *And it came to pass, when the children of Israel cried unto the Lord because of the Midianites,*

Testimony

The Midianites provided opposition to the Israelites as they journeyed toward the Promised Land. Who is providing opposition in your life as you journey with Christ? God called Gideon to overtake the Midianites. You have Jesus to take over the people that oppress you. Pray for those people to see Christ.

Mission

Getting closer and closer to Jesus is the most important thing in life. Don't let anyone oppress your walk with the Lord.

Daily Notes: _____

_____

_____

_____

_____

_____

_____

_____

_____

_____

_____

MORDECAI

Mordecai: the cousin and guardian of Esther who delivered the Jews from the destruction planned by Haman.

> **Ester 9:4** — *For Mordecai was great in the king's house, and his fame went all throughout all the provinces: for this man Mordecai waxed greater and greater.*

Testimony

Mordecai was concerned with saving his people and doing God's business. If Mordecai had been consumed with himself he would have failed. He kept his focus on serving others and doing what was right and acceptable in the sight of the Lord. Because of this, Mordecai received a great name and place in the king's house.

Mission

Be all about Jesus, because Jesus is all about you. Don't be concerned with yourself, focus on others.

Daily Notes: _____

_____

_____

_____

_____

_____

_____

_____

_____

MESSAGE

March 26

Message: a communication containing some information, news, advice, request, or the like, sent by messenger, telephone, email, or other means.

> **Daniel 5:5** — *In the same hour came fingers of a man's hand, and wrote over against the candlestick upon the plaster of the wall of the kings palace: and the king saw the part of the hand that wrote.*

Testimony

Seeing the forth fingers, the king's countenance was changed and his thoughts troubled him. He shook all over. Then he did exactly what he had done time and time before; he forgot. He called in all the astrologers and everyone that he thought could interpret until the queen reminded him of Daniel. Daniel had already helped him in the past. Daniel interpreted the writing. Daniel read the wall, saying, "God, whose hand thy breath is in, and whose ways you have not glorified."

Mission

Don't fall into the same trap King Nebuchadnezzar did. Don't forget the prayers God has already answered. Don't rely on anyone but Jesus to make known to you what he wants you to do.

Daily Notes: _____

_____

_____

_____

_____

_____

MIGHTY

Mighty: of great size; huge

Genesis 1:1 — *In the beginning God created the heaven and the earth.*

Testimony

There is a children's song that goes "He's got the whole world in His hands. He's got the whole wide world in His hands. He's got the whole world in His hands. He's got the whole world in His hands." Think about how mighty and strong Jesus hands are. They are tougher than nails and our sins. He carried the weight of the world in them. He still does. The Lord God is all mighty.

Mission

Remind yourself of whose mighty, strong, hands you are in.

Daily Notes: _____

_____

_____

_____

_____

_____

_____

_____

_____

_____

_____

MESHACH

March 28

Meshach: a companion of Daniel.

Daniel 3:16 — *Shadrach, Meshach, and Abed-nego, answered and said to the king, O Nebuchadnezzar, we are not careful to answer thee in this matter.*

Testimony

The three were bold to the king. God saved the three from the fiery furnace Nebuchadnezzar threw them in; but do we know anything about the three men individually? The three are always mentioned together. Could you imagine if one of them got prideful? There have been several bands break up because one person got the spot light or another person wanted it. These three men are mentioned in scripture as a group — never individually. This is the only time we hear about them in scripture. What if they wanted the spot light alone? What if they didn't want to do things as a group? What if their eyes were fixed on themselves and not Jesus? If that were the case, we may have never read about them or their encouraging story in scripture.

Mission

Don't neglect the people God has placed you with. They are the people that God uses to build your relationship with Him. The spotlight is never about you, but it is always about Jesus.

Daily Notes: _____

_____

_____

_____

_____

MEDIATOR

Mediator: to occupy an intermediate place or position.

> **Hebrews 9:15** — *And for this cause he is the mediator of the new testament, that by means of death, for the redemption of the transgressions, that were under the first testament, they which are called might receive the promise of eternal inheritance.*

Testimony

The sacrifices of the Old Testament didn't get rid of sin. They just cover them for a period of time until you sin again. Jesus covered all the sins of the world at one time — now and forever. If you have accepted Jesus, then you have a mediator today that has paid for all your sins and has written your name down in the Book of Life. He has made a home for you in Heaven to enjoy with him for eternity.

Mission

Don't forget who covered your sins on the cross. If you try to pick up your past sins, you're a thief. They no longer belong to you, because Jesus took care of them on the cross. Leave your past sins alone. They are paid for.

Daily Notes: _____

_____

_____

_____

_____

_____

_____

MANIFESTED

Manifested: readily perceived by the eye or the understanding; evident; obvious; apparent; plain:

> **1 John 1:2** — *(For the life was manifested, and we have seen it, and bear witness, and shew unto you that eternal life, which was with the Father, and was manifested unto us;)*

Testimony

Does your life prove that Jesus is alive? Is Christ so manifested in your life that people can look and see the results of a fruit-bearing life for your savior? Jesus showed others the oneness of Himself and His father. Jesus' life manifested His Father at all times.

Mission

Make sure Jesus is manifested in your life.

Daily Notes: _____

_____

_____

_____

_____

_____

_____

_____

_____

_____

MARCH

March 31

Reflection of the month of March:

1 John 1:7 — *But if we walk in the light, as he is in the light, we have fellowship one with another, and the blood of Jesus Christ his Son cleanseth us from all sin.*

Testimony

What Jesus does, he does forever! He is the One who has made you new. He laid down your old man and created a new man — God-glorifying, forever covered by His blood, sins washed white as snow — you!

Mission

Thank Jesus for his ultimate sacrifice. Read over your favorite devotions from the month of March. Don't forget how great Jesus is and His sacrifice.

Daily Notes: _____

_____

_____

_____

_____

_____

_____

_____

_____

_____

_____

APOLOGIZE

April 1

Apologize: to offer an apology or excuse for some fault, insult, failure, or injury:

> **Matthew 5:44** — *But I say unto you, Love your enemies, bless them that curse you, do good to them that hate you, and pray for them which despitefully use you, and persecute you;*

Testimony

Even when we're not at fault, we still need to be the first to apologize. Based on this scripture, the love of God extends beyond our human capability. We need the Lord to work this kind of love through us. We need to be humble and love our enemies — those that are not always lovable. Do good to them that hate you. What Lord? Can He be serious? This is a love so deep that it's hard for us to comprehend. Pray that God will show us the love that Jesus wants us to have. Apologizing can be the first step in reconnecting a lost relationship.

Mission

Take your eyes off of you and put them on Jesus. Don't let pride get in your way of showing others the love of Christ. Pray to be able to see and understand this deep love.

Daily Notes: _____

_____

_____

_____

_____

_____

ASK

April 2

Ask: to request information about:

Matthew 21:22 — *And all things, whatsoever ye shall ask in prayer, believing, ye shall receive.*

Testimony

How should we pray? Pray as if you have already received what you are praying about. Jesus says, "believing ye shall receive." Thank Jesus, when praying. Thank Him for the prayers he is answering and the ones He will be answering. A friend of mine said to me, "Kayla, when you go to the altar at church, as soon as your knees hit the floor to pray, your needs have been met." Now every time I pray I remember my needs have already been met. It's really exciting, too! When I forget this story, Jesus stops me and says, "Just get on your knees." As soon as my knees hit the ground I remember my needs have been met.

I prayed and asked for Jesus to send me my soul mate. I prayed this prayer around Valentine's Day. Our church was having a Valentine's Day dinner and I had resigned to go alone. In the mean time, I prayed a fairy tale like prayer, "Lord, I would love for the love of my life to be there. I would love flowers and to go on a date." That night I went to the dinner and my future husband was there. Even more amazing, he was supposed to be working. His boat docked so he got off the boat for just one night — long enough for the dinner before he had to go back to work. This never happens in his line of work, but it happened that night. We went on a date and the next day he sent flowers to my work. Jesus is that good! I just asked and prayed a very corny, fairy tale like prayer. Jesus loves me — and He loves you — and He gave me my heart's desire when I asked.

Mission

In memory of Hank Gibson: "Just Ask!" Hank was a mighty man of the Lord. He led services at our church and every time we talked about our prayer requests and made our petitions known to the Lord, Hank would say, "in faith believing, people." Many times while leading the service, Hank would say, "Just ask! It's simple people. Don't make it any more complicated than it's supposed to be."

Daily Notes: _____

_____

_____

_____

_____

_____

_____

_____

_____

_____

_____

_____

_____

_____

_____

_____

_____

_____

_____

_____

_____

ANOINT

April 3

Anoint: to dedicate to the service of God.

> **James 5:14-15** — *Is any sick among you? Let him call for the elders of the church; and let them pray over him, anointing him with oil in the name of the Lord: And the prayer of faith shall save the sick, and the Lord shall raise him up; and if he have committed any sins, they shall be forgiven him.*

Testimony

A prayer of faith will save the sick. This is what Jesus tells us to do when we are sick — not that we *might* be healed, but that we *will* be healed. Jesus not only heals our sins, but He heals us physically as well. It is God's will that we be whole and healthy. We have had countless people healed by Jesus in our church — a woman and a man needing a heart transplant, a brain tumor, back injuries, cancer, and so much more. Jesus healed them! We read about that in scripture. I have good news...Jesus heals today, too.

Mission

When you're ill, read this chapter in James. Do what it says and know that Jesus says you will be healed.

Daily Notes: _____

_____

_____

_____

_____

_____

_____

AM

April 4

Am: 1st person singular present

Exodus 3:14 — *And God said unto Moses, I AM THAT I AM: and he said, Thus shalt thou say unto the children of Israel, I AM hath sent me unto you.*

Testimony

When Jesus called Moses to bring the people out of Egypt, Moses asked, "Lord, who do I tell them sent me?" God replied, "I AM THAT I AM." Tell them, "I AM hath sent me unto you." God is the One who acts and who makes all things clear. God is everything. It is God's promise to redeem us. It is God who says, "I AM" or "I WILL BE." It's God's promise that He is actively working out everything in our lives. If you have accepted Jesus, you are redeemed because of I AM.

Mission

Think of Jesus saying, "I AM everything. You can do anything through me because I AM LIVING IN YOU!"

Daily Notes: _____

_____

_____

_____

_____

_____

_____

_____

APPRECIATE

April 5

Appreciate: to value or regard highly; place a high estimate on:

Ruth 2:12 — *The Lord recompense thy work, and a full reward be given thee of the Lord God of Israel, under whose wings thou art come to trust.*

Testimony

Boaz appreciates Ruth's kindness and notices her, and especially how she treats her mother-in-law, Naomi. He recognizes this as an opportunity to do to Ruth as she has done unto her mother-in-law. He gives her protection and a life with him just as God does with us. Through Ruth, Boaz appreciates God in whom his young Moabitess had only recently come to trust.

Mission

Appreciate the little things in life because God turns the little things into big things.

Daily Notes: _____

_____

_____

_____

_____

_____

_____

_____

_____

_____

ABOUND

April 6

Abound: to occur or exist in great quantities or numbers:

2 Corinthians 9:8 — *And God is able to make all grace abound towards you; that ye, always having all sufficiency in all things, may abound to every good work.*

Testimony

God loves a cheerful giver. God will always give you more than you could ever give Him. He already gave His Son for you. What you give to Jesus will be given back unto you so that you will be blessed. Jesus will give you so much more that it will take care of your needs, plus you will have some left over to give to others. Jesus' blessings abound in us, through us, and around us. He has a storage building full of blessings bursting out the windows that He wants to give to us.

Mission

Be ready to abound in all the blessings Jesus has for you. Get in a position that Jesus can give you all that He wants, too.

Daily Notes: _____

_____

_____

_____

_____

_____

_____

_____

_____

ADORE

April 7

Adore: to regard with the utmost esteem, love, and respect; honor.

Psalm 100:4 — *Enter into his gates with thanksgiving, and into his courts with praise: be thankful unto him, and bless his name.*

Testimony

Sometimes when we pray, we give the Lord a list of our wants. This verse shows us how to enter His gates with thanksgiving and His courts with praise. Be thankful and bless His name. It's easy to pray, but sometimes we forget to praise the Lord for answering our prayers. The Lord should be adored for all He does for us.

I was driving our jeep with my cousin and the jeep quit. I immediately started praying, "Lord please let this jeep start!" The jeep started right back up and ran fine ever since that day. Looking back on the story, did I praise the Lord as hard as I prayed for the Lord to start the jeep? We can't forget to adore our Lord and praise Him for all He does.

Mission

Adore the Lord.

Daily Notes: _____

_____

_____

_____

_____

_____

_____

_____

ANTICIPATED

April 8

Anticipated: to expect; look forward to; be sure of:

> **2 Kings 9:23** — *And Joram turned his hands and fled, and said to Ahaziah, there is treachery, O Ahaziah.*

Testimony

Joram anticipated that he would be able to escape, but he didn't anticipate being caught off guard and it cost him his life. Sin equals death. We should learn from Joram and anticipate every situation. If we don't look forward and willingly enter into a sinful situation, we could end up like Joram — our death or someone else's.

Mission

Anticipate your life and daily decisions. Make sure they are Christ focused. If not, then anticipate the situation before going forward. You may need to flee in the opposite direction.

Daily Notes: _____

_____

_____

_____

_____

_____

_____

_____

_____

_____

AHAB

April 9

Ahab: a king of Israel and husband of Jezebel.

> **2 Kings 10:11** — *So Jehu slew all that remained in the house of Ahab in Jezreel, and all his great men, and his kinsfolks, and his priests, until he left him none remaining.*

Testimony

Ahab's seventy sons were killed. Wickedness will not be remembered or honored. You cannot find the graves of Jezebel or her husband, Ahab. Elijah's prophecy was fulfilled. We read in 1 Kings 21:23-24 that the dogs would eat them up if they died in the streets. If they died in the fields, the fowl of the air would eat them up. This is the result of constantly ignoring God. Don't continue to believe the lies of satan that says you have a better plan for your life than Jesus does. The house of Ahab never got to a point before death where they realized the truth. You have a chance to change your path. Don't be consumed by wickedness.

Mission

Live a life that's memorable. Leave a trail of Jesus everywhere you go.

Daily Notes: _____

_____

_____

_____

_____

_____

_____

AHAZIAH

April 10

Ahaziah: king of Judah

2 Kings 9:27 — *But when Ahaziah the king of Judah saw this, he fled by the way of the garden house. And Jehu followed after him, and said, smite him also in the chariot. And they did so at the going up to Gur, which is by Ibleam. And he fled to Megiddeo, and died there.*

Testimony

All we really know about Ahaziah in scripture was that he fled and hid. He was evil and he was encouraged by those around him to do evil. His life resulted in running and hiding for his life. We can't hide from God. He knows us and he knows our secret sins. Stop trying to hide or run away to different places like Ahaziah did. Look into your heart and don't hold any sin back from God. He paid for them all.

Mission

Stop running. Jesus died for those secret sins, too. Ask for forgiveness and move on.

Daily Notes: _____

_____

_____

_____

_____

_____

_____

_____

_____

A LOT

April 11

A lot: very much.

> **Psalms 1:3** — *And he shall be like a tree planted by the rivers of water, that bringeth forth his fruit in his season; his leaf also shall not wither; and whatsoever he doeth shall prosper.*

Testimony

The Lord knows the ways of the righteous and He WILL bless it — not that he *might,* but, that He *WILL*. Anything that we do for the Lord will be blessed a lot more than we think.

There is a cake shop out West that took a righteous stand for the Lord. They had threats against their business and things seemed to go wrong. They knew that they had done what was right in the sight of the Lord though. Because of their righteous stand, they were blessed a lot. Don't ever go with the way the wind blows or the way the world wants you to go. Go to the Word and see what Jesus says about the issue and go with that. Take a righteous stand for our Lord. The result is A LOT.

Mission

Be a tree planted by the water so that when the storms come, people can look at you and say, "They are in a storm, but the Lord has blessed them A LOT."

Daily Notes: _____

_____

_____

_____

_____

APPLE

Apple: symbol of what is most cherished,

> **Psalm 17:8** — *Keep me as the apple of the eye, hide me under the shadow of thy wings.*

Testimony

Just like we protect the pupil of our eyes, the Lord protects us that same way. God knows and protects the most sensitive part of us. We are protected under the shadow of his wings the same way a bird's wing casts a shadow on the ground.

I was at a park and watched a mother duck with all her baby ducks following her. They were tucked right under her wing where they felt protected. Isn't it good to know that you are under the shadow of God's wing? He will protect you and hold you.

Mission

Don't forget whose wings you're under. You are the apple of God's eye.

Daily Notes: _____

_____

_____

_____

_____

_____

_____

_____

_____

_____

ABIGAIL

April 13

Abigail: the wife of Nabal and later of David.

1 Samuel 25:18 — *Then Abigail made haste, and took two hundred loaves, and two bottles of wine, and five sheep ready dressed, and five measures of parched corn, and an hundred clusters of raisins, and two hundred cakes of figs, and laid them on donkeys.*

Testimony

Abigail was the wife of Nebal. He was an ill-tempered, drunken man. David heard that Nebal had ignored his request, and mocked him. So King David set out to kill Nebal because of his disrespect. But Nebal's wife was wise, beautiful, and intelligent. She showed David kindness and blessed him with her gifts, taking matters into her own hands so that David would spare her husband's life. Later, after he died, she became the wife of King David.

Sometimes if it's not our fault we still need to take care of those around us. Even though beautiful Abigail did nothing wrong, she did everything to spare her husband's and her family's lives.

Mission

Do what you can to keep the peace.

Daily Notes: _____

_____

_____

_____

_____

_____

ABIMELECH

April 14

Abimelech: a son of Gideon, who made a violent but futile attempt to become king of Shechem.

Judges 9:53 — *And a certain woman cast a piece of a millstone upon Abimelech's head, and all to break his skull.*

Testimony

Abimelech killed all 70 of his brothers, sisters, and half brothers and sisters. He didn't want anyone to stop him from obtaining what he wanted — the throne. His life ended because he got too close to the city's wall and a woman dropped a millstone on his head, killing him. He commanded his armor-bearer to kill him, so no one could say he died at the hand of a woman. This man, who killed and slaughtered many, died in the most embarrassing way at that time. Even though his armor-bearer did in fact thrust him with his sword, the truth was not covered up. He died trying to lie, the same way he lived his life.

Mission

Embrace the truth in your life. Do not live a lie. If you're believing that you're not worthy, not capable, or unable, you're believing a lie. The truth is, Jesus has made you worthy of all. You are an overcomer, capable, able, and worthy of all Christ wants you to become.

Daily Notes: _____

_____

_____

_____

_____

ANYTHING

April 15

Anything: anything whatever; something, no matter what.

2 Samuel 6:14 — *And David danced before the Lord with all his might; and David was girded with a linen ephod.*

Testimony

Anything that the Lord tells you to do, just do it. However you want to worship the Lord, just do it. David danced! David danced with all his might before the Lord. In today's society if someone started dancing with all their might for the Lord we might look at them strangely. Do you think that would bother them? It doesn't mention anyone dancing with David, but David is remembered forever in scripture as someone dancing before the Lord. Don't worry about man's reactions. Focus on anything that will bring God glory. Just do it.

We have a man that comes to our church and the Holy Spirit speaks to him. He will skip a little every now and then as he walks right up on stage, grabs the microphone, and sings his heart out to the Lord. He will shout, sing, and jump. He doesn't care about anything but serving the Lord to his fullest.

Mission

Do anything to bring glory to God.

Daily Notes: _____

_____

_____

_____

_____

ASA

April 16

Asa: a king of Judah,

1 Kings 15:14 — *But the high places were not removed: nevertheless Asa's heart was perfect with the Lord all the days of his life.*

Testimony

What a testimony to leave behind to your family and all the authority figures over you. Asa's heart was perfect with the Lord all the days of his life. My heart needs to be readjusted from time to time to line up with the Word of God. We need to pray for God to check our heart so it can line up perfectly with Him. We need to strive to leave the type of legacy that Asa left behind.

Mission

Pray that your heart would be made perfect with the Lord. Let the Lord change it.

Daily Notes: _____

_____

_____

_____

_____

_____

_____

_____

_____

_____

ABIJAM

April 17

Abijam: king of Judah

> **1 Kings 15:3-4** — *And he walked in all the sins of his father, which he had done before him: and his heart was not perfect with the Lord his God, as the heart of David his father. Nevertheless for David's sake did the Lord his God give him a lamp in Jerusalem, to set up his son after him, and to establish Jerusalem:*

Testimony

David did what was right in the sight of the Lord. Because of David, Abijam experienced posterity. Are you counting on other people to get you by? Abijam was. People only get you so far, but they can never accept salvation for you. While living on earth, Abijam experienced posterity, but what all did he miss out on because he lacked a relationship with the Lord? David had a perfect heart towards the Lord, so his son, Abijam, received blessings from the Lord. Because David did what was commanded of the Lord, his son received blessings from the Lord. Are you counting on and watching the blessings of others?

Mission

Get your heart perfect with the Lord so you can experience His blessings first hand. The Lord wants to give you blessings. Don't try to get them through someone else. The Lord has a blessing waiting just for you.

Daily Notes: _____

_____

_____

_____

ABUNDANCE

April 18

Abundance: overflowing fullness

1 Kings 18:44 — *And it came to pass at the seventh time, that he said, Behold, there ariseth a little cloud out of the sea, like a mans hand. And he said Go up, say unto Ahab, Prepare thy chariot, and get thee down, that the rain stop thee not.*

Testimony

Elijah knew an abundance of rain was coming. He told his servant to look. He looked seven times before he saw the rain coming. What if he gave up the first time? What if Elijah doubted the first time and assumed the rain wouldn't come? He didn't. He sent his servant to look seven times because he knew the rain was coming. We know what is coming when serving the Lord — blessings beyond measure, God's promises, Eternal Life, and so much more. Do we look once and give up? We need to be like Elijah. Never stop searching for the Lord but waiting patiently because goodness is coming from Him. Look for it.

Mission

Never give up looking, watching, and waiting for the blessings of the Lord. They are coming!

Daily Notes: _____

_____

_____

_____

_____

_____

AMALEKITES

April 19

Amalekites: a tribe that dwelt in Arabia Petraea.

1 Chronicles 4:43 — *And they smote the rest of the Amalekites that were escaped, and dwelt there unto this day.*

Testimony

Evil will not be rewarded. I'm sure some of the Amalekites thought they were off the hook once they escaped from David's attack. They found land and set up tents and lived peaceable. But once Hezekiah, king of Judah, found them, they were destroyed. You can't run and hide, and escape the evil you've done. There is only one thing that must be done and that's applying the blood of Jesus to those sins so that they are no longer held against you. This was the fate of a group of people ignoring Jesus.

Mission

Don't ignore Jesus.

Daily Notes; _____

_____

_____

_____

_____

_____

_____

_____

_____

AWARD

Award: something awarded

> **2 Timothy 4:7-8** — *I have fought a good fight, I have finished my course, I have kept the faith: Henceforth there is laid up on me a crown of righteousness, which the Lord, the righteous judge, shall give me at that day: and not to me only, but unto all them also that love his appearing.*

Testimony

If you can't say what Paul said, then get to the place where you can. Pray to Jesus that you can — through Him — fight the good fight with faith. Let Jesus equip you to finish the course. You don't want to miss the reward of his precious love.

Mission

Pray to live a life so that you will receive the reward — a crown of righteousness.

Daily Notes: _____

_____

_____

_____

_____

_____

_____

_____

_____

_____

_____

ANCHOR

April 21

Anchor: a person or thing that can be relied on for support, stability, or security; mainstay

> **Hebrews 6:19** — *Which hope we have as an anchor of the soul, both sure and stedfast, and which entereth into that within the veil.*

Testimony

Jesus is our anchor — the anchor to our souls. He is the support that reaches beyond anything we could do in or by ourselves. He is our everything and we are complete in Him. An anchor can be used in the sea to drop down to the deepest level of the ocean floor to keep the ship in place. Our anchor is Jesus. He has the deepest level of love for us and it reaches unto the highest Heaven, and all the way into the depth of the sea.

Mission

Remind yourself daily that your anchor is Jesus Christ. Throw your anchor into Jesus.

Daily Notes: _____

_____

_____

_____

_____

_____

_____

_____

ANNUALLY

April 22

Annually: living only one growing season

> **Acts 3:2** — *And a certain man lame from his mother's womb was carried, whom they laid daily at the gate of the temple which is called Beautiful, to ask alms of them that entered into the temple.*

Testimony

What good friends this man had! Someone had to carry him every day, not just periodically. Finally, one day he got more than he was asking for. He got healed and his life was changed forever.

Mission

Get to the place where Jesus can bless you daily, not just annually.

Daily Notes: _____

_____

_____

_____

_____

_____

_____

_____

_____

_____

_____

ARROW

April 23

Arrow: a slender, straight, generally pointed missile or weapon made to be shot from a bow and equipped with feathers at the end of the shaft near the nock, for controlling flight.

> **Psalm 127:4** — *As arrows in the hand of a mighty man; so are the children of the youth.*

Testimony

Our youth is the next generation! Whether you have your own kids or are just around them, you have a responsibility to them. This is how powerful Jesus describes them. We need to encourage them in the ways of the Lord. They are powerful instruments for the Lord. Jesus compares them to an arrow. An arrow is a weapon, and Jesus compares the youth to an arrow in the hand of a mighty man. How powerful! We need to encourage them in the ways of the Lord versus the ways of the world.

Mission

Make sure the youth you are surrounded by knows how precious and powerful they are in the Lord.

Daily Notes: _____

_____

_____

_____

_____

_____

_____

_____

_____

AMETHYST

April 24

Amethyst: a purple or violet quartz, used as a gem.

Proverbs 20:15 — *There is gold, and a multitude of rubies: but the lips of knowledge are a precious jewel.*

Testimony

No jewels, gold, or money; nothing can equal or measure up to the value of the lips that speak knowledge. Jewels are beautiful with beautiful colors that dazzle and shine. We are drawn to their appearance. How are your lips? How are the words you're speaking? Are your lips and words full of the knowledge of Jesus? What if your words had an appearance like gems? What color would they appear? Would they dazzle and shine? We have the choice to speak knowledge and truth. We also have the choice to speak death. What will you speak?

Mission

Think of your words as having color that shines. Make sure you're lighting up the world with the knowledge of Christ and speaking life.

Daily Notes: _____

_____

_____

_____

_____

_____

_____

_____

ALTER

April 25

Alter: to make or become different in some respect; change

> **Isaiah 43:18** — *Remember ye not the former things, neither consider the things of old.*

Testimony

If you have accepted Jesus, He has altered your heart. If you follow Him after you have accepted Him, He will alter every aspect of your life. Know that once you accept Jesus, your life and who you are will be altered every day to the perfect Will of God. Know who is altering every detail in your life and wait with hope and joy for everything that God does. It is for your good. Don't remember the old things or the former things. You're a new creature in Jesus. You're growing and altering everyday to become stronger in the Lord.

Mission

You are altering right now in Jesus. Believe it!

Daily Notes: _____

_____

_____

_____

_____

_____

_____

_____

_____

ALTAR

April 26

Altar: an elevated place or structure

Matthew 23:19 — *Ye fools and blind: for whether is greater, the gift, or the altar that sanctifieth the gift?*

Testimony

Bowing at the altar in your church is a place of change. You can lay your burdens down at the altar. You leave changed. Sometimes we pray at the altar and instead of leaving the burden there, we pick them up and remain the same. We drag the same things we are praying about with us instead of leaving them to Jesus. Jesus will meet you. Call upon His name. Know that you have been transformed because of Who met you at the altar. Your altar can be anywhere you meet with the Lord. Your altar might not look the same as mine. The power isn't in how the altar looks; it's in Whom you are praying to. Jesus will meet you at your altar when you humbly pray and bow before the Lord.

Mission

Go to the altar and leave changed.

Daily Notes: _____

_____

_____

_____

_____

_____

_____

_____

ABIDE

April 27

Abide: to remain; continue; stay

> **John 15:7** — *If ye abide in me, and my words abide in you, ye shall ask what ye will, and it shall be done unto you.*

Testimony

Abide in Jesus. Stay put. Throw your heart into the Lord. Jesus will keep it. He will not break it. Don't pick it up and run away from the Lord. Stay put and abide. Be one with the Lord. That is what Jesus wants from us. Choose to abide with Him saying, "I abide in you, Lord."

Mission

Abide with Jesus.

Daily Notes: _____

_____

_____

_____

_____

_____

_____

_____

_____

_____

_____

_____

AMMON

April 28

Ammon: another form of the name Ben: ammi, the son of Lot

> **Matthew 6:24** — *No man can serve two masters: for either he will hate the one, and love the other; or else he will hold to the one, and despise the other. Ye cannot serve God and mammon.*

Testimony

God cannot be divided between your loyalty to Him and your loyalty to your material possessions. God knows our hearts and wants all of it! The children of Ammon and Moab prayed in certain sanctuaries, but did not prevail. God knew their divided hearts. He knew they trusted in other things instead of Him. Today, what are we trusting in more than the Lord? During troubles, if you find yourself not coming to the Lord first, it could be you are trusting in yourself, or something else, instead of Him.

Mission

Trust Jesus and give him your whole heart. Do not be divided. Put Him first.

Daily Notes: _____

_____

_____

_____

_____

_____

_____

_____

AMALEK

April 29

Amalek: a nomadic tribe or nation descended from Amalek and hostile to Israel

> **Exodus 17:14** — *And the LORD said unto Moses, Write this for a memorial in a book, and rehearse it in the ears of Joshua: for I will utterly put out the remembrance of Amalek from under heaven.*

Testimony

The Amalekites were put out of the remembrance from the Lord. The cruel life they lived resulted in them no longer being remembered under heaven. David smote those that escaped attacks until not one cruel Amalek remained. If you've found yourself being cruel — taking advantage of those that are weaker around you — then stop now and turn it around. As long as we're breathing we have a chance to make things right with other people and the Lord. Don't take being cruel lightly.

Mission

Make sure the only advantage you're taking is every opportunity to serve the Lord that comes your way.

Daily Notes: _____

_____

_____

_____

_____

_____

_____

_____

APRIL

April 30

Reflection of the month of April:

Jeremiah 48: 7 — *For because thou has trusted in thy works and in thy treasures, thou shalt also be taken: and Chemosh shall go forth into captivity with his priests and his princes together.*

Testimony

Don't trust in your own works, finances, relationships, or a status to get you by. What you put your trust in will eventually hold you captive.

Mission

Reflect on the month of April what has taken you captive? If it's anything other than Christ, let it go. Let Jesus captivate every area of your life. Trust in Him.

Daily Notes: _____

_____

_____

_____

_____

_____

_____

_____

_____

_____

_____

MAY

May: permission

1 Peter 5:8 — *Be sober, be vigilant; because your adversary the devil, as a roaring lion, walketh about, seeking whom he may devour.*

Testimony

There is a man in our church that is so full of wisdom. My spirit always bears witness with his, and every time he leads the service, I know the Lord is speaking directly to me. One day he spoke on this verse. He pointed out that the devil can't just take our joy. He has to ask our permission. The scripture says, "whom he MAY devour." Satan cannot take anything away from the child of the King. We have to give it to him.

Mission

Don't give satan any permission. Be joyful and rejoice at all times. Look to God who is working things out for His glory and your good.

Daily Notes: _____

_____

_____

_____

_____

_____

_____

_____

_____

MISSION

May 2

Mission: any important task or duty that is assigned

John 9:25— *He answered and said, Whether he be a sinner or no, I know not: one thing I know, that, whereas I was blind, now I see.*

Testimony

We were once blind, on a mission of destruction. If you have accepted Christ, you are now on a mission to see Him in all things and for people to see Jesus through you. You were blind but now you see. Don't you see how good Jesus is? Our mission is to show the love of Christ and spread the Gospel to all the nations. Don't neglect your mission. There are blind people waiting and wanting to see Jesus. Help them be able to say, "I was blind but now I see."

Mission

Our mission is Jesus.

Daily Notes: _____

_____

_____

_____

_____

_____

_____

_____

_____

_____

MANUFACTURE

May 3

Manufacture: to work up (material) into form for use:

> **Genesis 2:7** — *And the Lord God formed man of the dust of the ground, and breathed into his nostrils the breath of life; and man became a living soul.*

Testimony

Only Jesus can take dust from the ground and manufacture a soul. Stop limiting Jesus. He can manufacture any situation in your life and put it to good use if you will give it to him. Stop trying to manufacture different areas of your life. Seek Jesus. Jesus is the only one who can breathe life into your dead situations. The dust on the ground became a living soul. How awesome is our God! Nothing is impossible for Him! Let Him manufacture every aspect of your life. Jesus will use anything and everything you give Him.

Mission

Who is your manufacturer? If it's Jesus, live like it!

Daily Notes: _____

_____

_____

_____

_____

_____

_____

_____

_____

MERCY

May 4

Mercy: compassionate or kindly forbearance shown toward an offender, an enemy, or other person in one's power; compassion, pity, or benevolence.

> **Psalm 23:6** — *Surely goodness and mercy shall follow me all the days of my life: and I will dwell in the house of the Lord forever.*

Testimony

We are a favored people of the Lord. Jesus is our protector and provider. We are His sheep; He is our Shepherd. Goodness and mercy will follow us all the days of our lives when we are relying on the mercy of the Lord. Show that mercy to everyone. A man in our church always says, "Sometimes we are the only Bible lost people will read." Keep that in mind as you live your day-to-day life. People need to see the mercy of our compassionate, merciful Lord.

Mission

Trust God and brag on Jesus.

Daily Notes: _____

_____

_____

_____

_____

_____

_____

_____

MISS

Miss: to fail to take advantage of:

> **Philippians 3:13-14** — *Brethren, I count not myself to have apprehended: but this one thing I do, forgetting those things which are behind, and reaching forth unto those things which are before, I press toward the mark for the prize of the high calling of God in Christ Jesus.*

Testimony

Pursue the goal to know Christ. Forget about the past. Don't let past guilt or situations stop you from experiencing all that Christ is. The things in the future are far better than anything in our past. Our goal is to draw closer to Jesus every day. You don't want to miss out on all the good things Jesus has for you. It would blow our minds if we truly knew all the Lord wanted to give us and all the blessings he wanted to pour out on us. So let's get them! Let's get to a place to receive all that Jesus has for us. Stop limiting God and yourself. Take advantage of all that Jesus is. Take advantage of the Word and all the power in it.

Mission

Have a Jesus goal every day. Don't miss out!

Daily Notes: _____

_____

_____

_____

_____

_____

_____

MIRACLE

May 6

Miracle: such an effect or event manifesting or considered as a work of God.

> **John 2:7** — *Jesus saith unto them, Fill the waterpots with water. And they filled them up to the brim.*

Testimony

Jesus' miracles always had a purpose and brought Him glory. Wouldn't it be nice if we could say everything we did in life did that also? Jesus had them bring him water pots that were usually used for washing feet. Isn't that like Jesus to use something unusable and turn it around for His glory? I love how Jesus takes things the world would look over and uses it for miracles. Whatever Jesus recreates is always better than it was and always better than anything man can do, just like the miracle of turning water into wine. Jesus takes us and turns a sinner into a saint. We were once unusable in our sin, but Jesus took us — just like he took the water pots with ordinary water — and made us a miracle, working for His glory.

Mission

You are a miracle of Jesus! Let him take the water pots in your life and turn them into miracles, testifying of His greatness!

Daily Notes: _____

_____

_____

_____

_____

MISMANAGE

May 7

Mismanage: to manage incompetently or dishonestly

> **Job 33:12** — *Behold, in this thou art not just: I will answer thee, that God is greater than man.*

Testimony

You cannot mismanage what God has given you. You cannot pray continuously for something, but then do nothing to help the situation. God has given us a life to live for Him with blessings, promises, and His Word. Job did not mismanage his life or what God had given him. He suffered greatly, and the majority of the crowd wanted him to complain in his sufferings. Instead, he stuck to what was true. Job praises God for His greatness. When his life was at stake, he continued to glorify God. As a result of Job managing what God had given him correctly, God gave him more.

Mission

Let Jesus manage your life.

Daily Notes: _____

_____

_____

_____

_____

_____

_____

_____

_____

_____

MIX

Mix: to combine, unite, or join:

> **Matthew 9:17** — *neither do men put new wine into old bottles: else the bottles break, and the wine runneth out, and the bottles perish: but they put new wine into new bottles, and both are preserved.*

Testimony

You cannot mix old wine and new wine or the fermentation of the new wine would be too much for the worn out, old wineskin and the bottles would break. Jesus came to give us grace. Grace didn't fit into the religious economy. Grace broke those laws and set us free from the law. Jesus fulfilled the law for us.

Jesus puts in us His spirit when we accept Him. After you've become a new creature in Christ, don't run back to the old sin. It does not belong to you. You can't put the new wine into an old wineskin. You cannot mix the two. They don't belong together — just like you and sin. Jesus paid for that sin on the cross. It does not belong to you. I encourage you, if you have sin in your new life with Christ, give it to Jesus and allow Him to break the chains. The price has already been paid.

Mission

Don't mix things that shouldn't be mixed.

Daily Notes: _____

_____

_____

_____

_____

MATCH

Match: a slender piece of wood, cardboard, or other flammable material tipped with a chemical substance that produces fire when rubbed on a rough or chemically prepared surface.

> **1 Kings 18:38-39** — *Then the fire of the Lord fell, and consumed the burnt sacrifice, and the wood, and the stones, and the dust, and licked up the water that was in the trench. And when all the people saw it, they fell on their faces: and they said, The Lord, he is the God; the Lord, he is the God.*

Testimony

They didn't need a match! Don't you realize to start a fire you don't need a match either! You have Jesus Christ living inside of you! Call upon His name! Let Him consume the burnt sacrifices in your life that don't point towards Him. We all have things in our lives that don't point directly to Christ. We need to adjust those things so that everything we do gives God glory. If something in your life is not pointing to Christ, call upon the name of the Lord and let him consume it. Jesus and His consuming power is so strong that the fire will lick up the water in the trenches. Don't underestimate the power of Christ.

Mission

Be consumed.

Daily Notes: _____

_____

_____

_____

MADE

May 10

Made: simple past tense and past participle of make.

Genesis 1:27 — *So God created man in his own image, in the image of God created he him; male and female created he them.*

Testimony

Jesus created us in His own perfect image. As long as we're looking to Jesus as our maker — the One who made us — we will be complete in Him, lacking nothing. We will have peace in the midst of storms.

I was driving to meet a friend for dinner one day and a preacher came on the radio, and he said, "You can't build without a builder. You can't have a creation without a creator." He looked in his wallet and said, "The money didn't just appear. I had to make it." We were made by Jesus to be complete in Him, lacking nothing.

Mission

Jesus doesn't make junk, and He made you.

Daily Notes: _____

_____

_____

_____

_____

_____

_____

_____

_____

MUST

May 11

Must: to be obliged or bound to by an imperative requirement:

John 3:4 — *Nicodemus saith unto him, how can a man be born when He is old? Can he enter the second time into his mother's womb, and be born?*

Testimony

You must be born again. Nicodemus was confused thinking of a physical birth instead of a spiritual birth. Being born again is a spiritual change that allows Jesus to come into your heart and change you from the inside out. The only way to enter into Heaven, and to be born again, is to believe Jesus is who He says He is. He died on the cross for your past, present, and future sins, and is coming again. Whoever calls upon His name shall be saved. After you have been born again, don't use your new birth as fireproof insurance. Don't stay a baby in Christ. Instead, let Jesus change and grow you to be more like Him.

Mission

Grow each day in Jesus. It's a must.

Daily Notes: _____

_____

_____

_____

_____

_____

_____

_____

MEAL

May 12

Meal: one of these regular occasions or times for eating food.

1 Kings 17:16 — *And the barrel of meal wasted not, neither did the cruse of the oil fail, according to the word of the LORD, which he spake by Elijah.*

Testimony

It was the woman and her son's last meal — the only thing they had left. She worried and tried to tell Elijah, "This is my last meal." Elijah told her, "Fear not. Go and make my meal first. Then make one for you and your son." Her faith was tested. When our faith is tested, we have to know that if we remain faithful, it brings glory to God. It's good for us and everyone is affected by it. So the woman did all that Elijah told her to do, and she was blessed for it. God provided. God will bless your little bit, when you give it to Him. All the woman had was a little bit, but God took it and she never ran out again. There was always more.

Mission

Take comfort in the fact that God will do and has already done everything for you.

Daily Notes: _____

_____

_____

_____

_____

_____

_____

MOUTH

May 13

Mouth: the opening through which an animal or human takes in food.

> **Jonah 1:8-9** — *Then said they unto him, Tell us, we pray thee, for whose cause this evil upon us; what is thine occupation? And whence comest thou? What is thy country? And of what people art thou? And he said unto them, I am a Hebrew; and I fear the Lord, the God of heaven, which hath made the sea and the dry land.*

Testimony

What words are coming out of your mouth? The world will ask us all kinds of questions based on our occupation, family, background, and relationships. How will we answer? Jonah ignored their questions because he had a better answer. He told them the most important thing about himself. "I fear the Lord," said Jonah. Then he goes on to tell them who God is. How do you explain yourself to people?

Mission

Let your words that come out of your mouth show who you believe in and what's most important to you.

Daily Notes: _____

_____

_____

_____

_____

_____

_____

MEAN

May 14

Mean: offensive, selfish, or unaccommodating; nasty; malicious:

Matthew 5:44 — *But I say unto you, Love your enemies, bless them that curse you, do good to them that hate you, and pray for them which despitefully use you, and persecute you;*

Testimony

A man in our church made a hilarious comment once. He said, "How many of you have ever sent a present to your enemy?" This verse shows us just how serious Jesus is about us loving others. Only through Christ is this kind of love possible. By showing the love of Christ we can win people to Jesus. This kind of love is only possible by having Jesus love through us.

Mission

Don't be mean. According to this verse you should always show the love of God.

Daily Notes: _____

_____

_____

_____

_____

_____

_____

_____

_____

MAYBE

May 15

Maybe: perhaps; possibly

1 Corinthians 7:14 — *For the unbelieving husband is sanctified by the wife, and the unbelieving wife is sanctified by the husband: else were your children unclean; but now they are holy.*

Testimony

There is no such thing as "maybe Jesus saving you; or maybe His promises coming through; or maybe Jesus hearing and answering your prayers." These things are certain, concrete, and one hundred percent. If the Word said these are *certain,* there is no *maybe* about it. Getting stuck in the *maybe* mind set is a lie from satan. There is nothing *maybe* about Jesus. But there is a *maybe* about us. We have the choice, just like the unbelieving husband and wife. Together they are more likely to become converted, but the choice is a *maybe*. Don't *maybe* around with Jesus. He didn't *maybe* around with you when He chose to die for you.

Mission

Don't get caught in a *maybe* mindset.

Daily Notes: _____

_____

_____

_____

_____

_____

_____

MOOD

May 16

Mood: an emotional tone or general attitude.

2 Corinthians 10:5 — *Casting down imaginations, and every high thing that exalteth itself against the knowledge of God, and bringing into captivity every thought to the obedience of Christ;*

Testimony

Paul in prison shouldn't be in a better mood than me. We find ourselves in different moods sometimes. Sometimes we know why; other times it just overcomes us. Paul tells us to bring every thought captive to the Lord. In doing this, wouldn't we then know if our mood was from God or not? If it's not good, it's not from God. Jesus doesn't desire us to be overtaken by our moods, but rather overcome them and rejoice always in Him. Jesus is bigger than our moods.

Mission

Take every thought captive. If your mood doesn't line up with the Word of God, let Christ fix it.

Daily Notes: _____

_____

_____

_____

_____

_____

_____

_____

MORE

May 17

More: additional or further

John 15:5 — *For without me ye can do nothing.*

Testimony
Why do we always think we can do more than the Lord? Jesus tells us that you cannot do anything; in fact, you can do nothing without me. Why would we want to do anything without the Lord anyways? Sometimes we think we know best. We think we know more than the Lord. We see what is right in front of us while Jesus sees the entire game plan — beginning to end. Trust in Jesus who sees every step you're currently taking. He will direct us in the most perfect way into His Glory and blessings that He has prepared for us.

I had a dog named Charlie, who I was crazy about. I was getting ready to go to Haiti so I put the responsibility of Charlie's care on everyone else while I got ready to go. I was temporarily living with my parents, so my dad had to find her another home. I was so worried. I prayed and prayed for Charlie. Years went by. When I got married, I started thinking about Charlie again — which made me think about getting another dog. I prayed for Charlie over and over again. She was a very big dog, and I had prayed that she had found a home on a farm with people who loved her.

One day, while driving my jeep down some old country back road, I saw a dog running through a field on a farm. The dog looked just like Charlie. I stopped and the dog ran over to me. It was Charlie! She still had the collar on that I had given her. She was on a farm and had a loving family. A little boy came out of his house and was calling her 'Annabelle.' The Lord had answered my prayers for Charlie. The next few days were hard since I had seen her, but I knew God was so good in doing more than I could ever have imagined for her.

I am a substitute teacher and teach at several different schools. One day as I was thinking about Charlie, a boy walked into my classroom. It was the little boy that was her current owner. We talked about Charlie/Annabelle all day. God is amazing. He will always do more than you could ever imagine.

Mission
Trust more.

Daily Notes: _____

_____

_____

_____

_____

_____

_____

_____

_____

_____

_____

_____

_____

_____

_____

_____

_____

_____

_____

_____

_____

_____

_____

_____

ME

May 18

Me: the objective case of I

> **Judges 6:16** — *And the Lord said to him, "Surely I will be with you, and you shall defeat the Midiaites as one man."*

Testimony

A friend of mine from church sent this scripture to me and said, "Me, as ONE man in Christ, He will defeat them!" Jesus did it with Gideon; and he can do it with us, too. Understand the power in Jesus. Most of us underestimate this power in Christ. We can do all things through Christ. This verse is proof of the power of what one man can do in Christ. You might be thinking, "Just me...what can I do?" You can do nothing without Jesus; but with Jesus, you can do all things. Let this verse encourage you to see that "just you, in Christ" can move mountains, defeat armies, and lead people to everlasting life!

Mission

Don't think of yourself and situations as "just me." Think of yourself as "me, in Jesus Christ!"

Daily Notes: _____

_____

_____

_____

_____

_____

_____

MIGHT

May 19

Might: physical strength

> **Zechariah 4:6** — *Then He answered and spake unto me, saying This is the word of the Lord unto Zerubbabel, saying, Not by might, nor by power, but by spirit, saith the Lord of hosts.*

Testimony

The Lord gave Zechariah several visions to encourage the people to continue building the temple, announcing God's glory and anticipating His blessings. In this verse Jesus reminds us that it's not by our might or power that we accomplish anything. It's by His Spirit. We will fail and our flesh will fail, if we think we are capable of living this life without Jesus. Is *your* might enough? Is *your* power enough? We need the Holy Spirit dwelling inside of us. The only thing we were created to do is to bring God glory. It's not about us at all.

Mission

Get in tune completely with the Holy Spirit. Stop relying on yourself. Instead, rely on the One who created you for His glory. Rely on Jesus and His never-failing might.

Daily Notes: _____

_____

_____

_____

_____

_____

_____

MAKE

Make: to move or proceed in a particular direction:

Romans 4:19 — *And being not weak in faith, he considered not his own body now dead, when he was about an hundred years old, neither yet the deadness of Sarah's womb;*

Testimony

Abraham had to make an effort to not have a doubtful mind and not consider his age or Sarah's womb. We have to make an effort not to look at our circumstances. Instead, glorify God and don't stagger at His promises. His promises are sure and God is faithful. We have to be willing to put our faith into action. We have to make an effort.

I went to a Christian concert by a group — called "Winter Jam" — that travels around. My friend and I went but we couldn't get in because the show was sold out. However, with all the willing Christians making an effort to come out for the concert, "Winter Jam" put on a little concert in the lobby.

I was in church after this and the Lord laid a song on my heart. After I sang it, a little girl said, "They didn't sing that one at "Winter Jam." My reply was, "I heard it in the lobby. We didn't make it in." Right then the Lord started speaking to me saying, "When you make the effort, I will bless it." I only made it as far as the lobby, but I made the effort and God blessed me for it.

Mission

Go where you will get a blessing from the Lord. Go! If you only make it to the lobby, God will still be there and will bless your efforts when you're focused on Him.

Daily Notes: _____

_____

MESSIAH

May 21

Messiah: Jesus Christ

John 1:41 — *He first findeth his own brother Simon, and saith unto him, We have found the Messias, which is being interpreted, the Christ.*

Testimony

They found the Messiah. Have you found the Messiah? Have you found Jesus Christ? Maybe you're saved and have accepted Jesus as your personal Lord and Savior. Have you found Jesus in every area of your life or is he missing in some areas? Do you need to find Jesus in every aspect of your life? Yes!

You need to be showing Jesus in every aspect of your life — at work, school, wherever the Lord has you. He has you where he wants you to bring Him glory. You're where you're at for a reason! Find the Messiah where you are!

Mission

Don't lose sight as to why we are here. Find the Messiah. Find Jesus in every area of your life.

Daily Notes: _____

_____

_____

_____

_____

_____

_____

_____

MAJESTY

May 22

Majesty: supreme greatness or authority; sovereignty:

> **Psalm 21:5** — *His glory is great in thy salvation: honor and majesty has thou laid upon him.*

Testimony

This is God's strength and we should be rejoicing in it. Jesus showed His majesty at the cross. They certainly didn't treat Him like majesty when He was nailed, beaten, and crushed for us. Jesus did that for you. Jesus embraced the cross for us. Jesus embraced the cross "for the joy set before him." That joy was us. In the midst of being crucified, Jesus looked up and said, "Father, forgive them. They know not what they do."

Mission

Don't forget the sacrifice that was made.

Daily Notes: _____

_____

_____

_____

_____

_____

_____

_____

_____

_____

MEDITATION

May 23

Meditation: continued or extended thought; reflection; contemplation.

Psalm 19:14 — *Let the words of my mouth, and the meditation of my heart, be acceptable in thy sight, O Lord, my strength, and my redeemer.*

Testimony

This is a prayer we need to pray. Our words speak life or death; curses or blessings. Our mouth and the words we speak also keep our souls from trouble. In order for our words to be acceptable, our hearts have to be made acceptable in the sight of the Lord. Out of our heart springs wells of living waters if we make our words and meditations acceptable to Him. As soon as we stop praying this prayer or caring about the issues of our heart or the words we speak, the enemy will move in. Give God control and let him strengthen your heart and mouth and make it acceptable in His sight, bringing Him glory.

Mission

Pray this prayer every day. Look for opportunities to speak about Jesus rather than the things of this world.

Daily Notes: _____

_____

_____

_____

_____

_____

_____

MEASURING

May 24

Measuring: to serve as the measure of

Zechariah 2:1 — *I lifted up mine eyes again, and looked and behold a man with a measuring line in his hand.*

Testimony

Zechariah had a vision of a man with a measuring line. He was measuring Jerusalem and the Lord spoke to him and said, "I will be unto her a wall of fire round about, and will be the glory in the midst of her." God will be our protector. Just like a measuring line measures from a starting point to an ending point and everything in between, God has his outstretched hand over all the boundaries and will be glorified. Jesus has covered us from the beginning to the end — not just in certain situations, but in every aspect of our lives until eternity. God is big and His outstretched hand will protect us.

Mission

Put your future in the hands of your protector. Jesus works all things out for your good. His love for you is not capable to being measured because it's never-ending — never gives up and never runs out.

Daily Notes: _____

_____

_____

_____

_____

_____

_____

MOTIVATION

Motivation: the act or an instance of motivating, or providing with a reason to act in a certain way:

> **Zechariah 10:12** — *And I will strengthen them in the Lord; and they shall walk up and down in his name, saith the Lord.*

Testimony

The Lord will motivate and strengthen his people and direct them in the way they should go. The theme of Zechariah is to motivate the people to rebuild the temple and show them that they are an important part of God's plan for displaying His glory to the future nations. Should our goals not be the same? Should we not be motivating people like the Lord is doing here through Zechariah? People often times know what they are doing is wrong. We need to motivate them in the ways of the Lord and seek instruction from the Lord on how to live a life that will bring God glory.

Mission

Be a motivator and provide Godly motivation to all those you see.

Daily Notes: _____

_____

_____

_____

_____

_____

_____

MARVELOUS

Marvelous : superb; excellent; great:

> **Psalm 118:23-24** — *This is the Lord's doing, it is marvelous in our eyes. This is the day which the Lord hath made; we will rejoice and be glad in it.*

Testimony

We should be praising the Lord daily for His marvelous good works. Scripture tells us to rejoice because this is the day the Lord has made — every day, not just when you feel like it or when things are going your way. There is beauty in every day that the Lord has given you. Look around and find His marvelous works. Look in His Word and see how marvelous and faithful our living Savior is.

Mission

Praise the Lord and rejoice in your salvation. View every day as a gift from God, because it is.

Daily Notes: _____

_____

_____

_____

_____

_____

_____

_____

_____

_____

MOON

May 27

Moon: the earth's natural satellite, orbiting the earth at a mean distance of 238,857 miles (384,393 km) and having a diameter of 2160 miles (3476 km).

> **Psalm 104:19** — *He appointed the moon for seasons: the sun knoweth his going down.*

Testimony

This is just one of God's marvelous creations that we should praise Him for. How complicated is the definition of the moon? The moon works to keep the Earth in orbit and greatly affects all living things on Earth. God is in everything because he created it all. He is our wonderful Creator. The Lord worked out every detail — to the second — of how the moon was going to orbit around the earth. Just like the moon and everything it does, Jesus is working out every detail to the finest in our lives as well. We only see right in front of us while Jesus sees the entire picture. He cares about every little detail. He not only cares about our needs, but also our wants. He is working out every detail to the finest in our lives so everything works perfectly and gives Him glory.

Mission

Trust Jesus in the details. He will make it work.

Daily Notes: _____

_____

_____

_____

_____

_____

MUSIC

May 28

Music: appreciation of or responsiveness to musical sounds or harmonies:

> **2 Samuel 6:14** — *And David danced before the Lord with all his might; and David was girded with a linen ephod.*

Testimony

David's response was to dance and praise the Lord. However you choose to worship the Lord, let it come from your heart. I've heard it said that worshipping the Lord is just giving back to the Lord the breath that He has given us. So whether you worship Jesus through song, instruments, music, or dancing; do it all with a heart devoted to praising God and thanking Him for all He has done.

Mission

Let your response to music be directed towards Christ instead of who is playing, what song is on, or who is around you.

Daily Notes: _____

_____

_____

_____

_____

_____

_____

_____

_____

_____

MOURNS

May 29

Mourns: to feel or express sorrow or grief.

2 Samuel 1: 12 — *And they mourned, and wept, and fasted until even, for Saul, and for Jonathan his son, and for the people of the Lord, and for the house of Israel; because they were fallen by the sword.*

Testimony

Earlier in David's life, Saul had been trying to kill him. David had escaped death as he followed the direction from the Lord. When Saul died, David mourned for him. Only Jesus can take a person who has wronged us and give us new respect for them. Saul was appointed by the Lord and David knew this. When given the chance to kill Saul, David honored the Lord. He obeyed His commands even when he knew Saul wanted to kill him.

Mission

Let Jesus heal your broken relationships so you can give Him glory like he did with David and Saul.

Daily Notes: _____

_____

_____

_____

_____

_____

_____

_____

MORDECAI

May 30

Mordecai: the cousin and guardian of Esther who delivered the Jews from the destruction planned by Haman.

Ester 10:3 — *For Mordecai the Jew was next unto King Ahasuerus, and great among the Jews, and accepted of the multitude of his brethren, seeking the wealth of his people, and speaking peace to all his seed.*

Testimony

All the greatness we read in the above scripture didn't just happen for Mordecai. At one point, Mordecai and all the Jews were being threatened. Mordecai was honored with a higher position from the king for how he had lived his life by putting others before himself. The result was a blessed life for him and his people. Peace for everyone.

One time I was debating about having a yard sale to make some extra money. A woman approached me saying, "How much money for everything?" I thought that was strange so I asked, "Why?" She explained that she liked some things herself, but knew of a family in need.

Instantly the devil started chattering. He said, "Look at all these things you have paid for. This is a lot of stuff!" Then the Lord spoke to me and said, "You can be greedy or give it all in My Name." So I gave her everything for free. She took two truckloads. If I would have sold everything, my plan was to get a small, flat screen TV for my bedroom.

The woman texted me and said, "Since you gave me everything for free, I have a flat screen TV for you if you would like it." Praise the Lord. The exact thing I was going to buy with the money, I got. I ended up getting an even better TV than I had planned! The Lord not only gives us what we need, but also gives us our heart's desires. The Lord worked that out perfectly. I didn't have to use my time having my sale to get the money I needed. I was obedient and gave it all. I did what Jesus said to do. He provided for me just like he did for Mordecai. He'll do this for you, too.

Mission

Trust and obey.

Daily Notes: _____

_____

_____

_____

_____

_____

_____

_____

_____

_____

_____

_____

_____

_____

_____

_____

_____

_____

_____

_____

_____

_____

MAY

May 31

Reflection of the month of May:

Ruth 2:16 — *And let fall also some of the handfuls of purpose for her, and leave them, that she may glean them, and rebuke her not.*

Testimony

Boaz showed favor on Ruth and told his young men to do the same for Ruth. Think of the favor God has given to you.

We have a running joke in my church. A person will say, "I'm God's favorite." God is so good to us and everything He does is for us. Truly, there is some truth behind that joke! We are a favored people of God. He loves us.

Mission

Reflect on this month. Think of God's outstretched hand and favor upon you. Think of the times and moments when God showed you His love. Wake up and be thankful for God's favor. Thank Him!

Daily Notes: _____

_____

_____

_____

_____

_____

_____

_____

_____

JONAH

June 1

Jonah: a Minor Prophet who, for his impiety, was thrown overboard from his ship and swallowed by a large fish, remaining in its belly for three days before being cast up onto the shore unharmed.

> **Jonah 1:8-9** — *Then said they unto him, Tell us, we pray thee, for whose cause this evil upon us; What is thine occupation? And whence comest thou? What is thy country? And of what people art thou? And he said unto them, I am an Hebrew; and I fear the LORD, the God of heaven, which hath made the sea and the dry land.*

Testimony

Jonah's answer was better than their questions. So, when Jonah replied, he told them the most important thing about who he was. People may ask us similar questions. Sometimes we miss the most important thing we have to offer — that's Jesus.

Mission

Always answer with Jesus.

Daily Notes: _____

_____

_____

_____

_____

_____

_____

_____

JOB

Job: a piece of work, especially a specific task done as part of the routine.

> **Mark 16:15** — *And he said unto them, Go ye into all the world, and preach the gospel to every creature.*

Testimony

Make what Jesus commands you to do part of your daily routine. You wouldn't miss going to work because you have a job to do. As a follower of Jesus, He commands you to do certain things as well. We need to take that seriously and treat it like it's our job, because it is.

Mission

Adjust your routine so that Jesus comes first. No job is more important than doing what God commands us to do.

Daily Notes: _____

_____

_____

_____

_____

_____

_____

_____

_____

_____

_____

JUNCTION

June 3

Junction: an act of joining; combining.

Ecclesiastes 3:11 — *He hath made everything beautiful in His time: also He hath set the world in their hearts, so that no man can find out the work that God maketh from the beginning to the end.*

Testimony

God has designed you and placed within you a desire for eternity so you cannot be satisfied with anything but Him. When you find yourself frustrated or tired, could it be that you're trying to fill that God-shaped design with things that aren't of God? He designed you to be in conjunction with Him. He loves us that much! What you're trying to fill was created for Jesus. The loneliness you may feel in your heart, let Jesus fill it up. Let this motivate you to not be afraid to tell others about Jesus because He has given them this same desire. Realize that none of us will function right until we are in conjunction with Jesus.

Mission

Get in conjunction with Jesus.

Daily Notes: _____

_____

_____

_____

_____

_____

_____

_____

JUDE

June 4

Jude: a book of the New Testament.

Jude 1:24-25 — *Now unto him that is able to keep you from falling, and to present you faultless before the presence of his glory with exceeding joy, to the only wise God our savior, be glory and majesty, dominion and power, both now and ever. Amen.*

Testimony

The book of Jude only consists of one chapter right before Revelations. It is a reaffirming and constant reminder of how we're kept with Jesus, reminding us to stay in God's love. The above scripture is comforting. If you have found yourself falling or stumbling, isn't it great to know that Jesus is able to pick us up, hold us, and keep us from falling, over and over again? Jesus sets us apart, but from the world. Not only does He set us apart but He keeps us. We are kept by Jesus. He holds us and loves us. Seek God's mercy and receive peace, love, and all that Jesus has to offer. You can personally trust your Savior, Jesus Christ.

Mission

Read Jude.

Daily Notes: _____

_____

_____

_____

_____

_____

_____

JEHOSHAPHAT

June 5

Jehoshaphat: the king of Judah.

> **2 Chronicles 20:6** — *And said, O LORD God of our fathers, art not thou God in heaven? And rulest not thou over all the kingdoms of the heathen? And in thine hand is there not power and might, so that none is able to with stand thee?*

Testimony

Jehoshaphat proves that not only is he a wise King, but he is a man of prayer. My husband felt God calling him to be a prayer warrior for our church. At first he questioned, "Me, a prayer warrior, God?" Jehoshaphat was a wise king and a man of prayer. Prayer is important and changes things. Prayer is direct communication with God — a conversation between you and the Lord. What better way to spend time with Jesus? Whatever God is calling you to do — whether it is a mighty leader, a prayer warrior, or the bell ringer in your church — it is important to the Body of Christ. Our job is to listen and be obedient. What if Jehoshaphat said, "I'm too busy! I'm a king! Humble myself and pray? Take time to pray, Lord?" Maybe Judah wouldn't have been given the promise of deliverance. What if my husband wouldn't have taken his calling seriously? Who knows who's being affected by your obedience? Trust Jesus with the things He is calling you to do. He is calling you for a reason and for such a time as this.

Mission

Trust God and do whatever He tells you to do. This life isn't about you. It is about doing everything God tells you to do with no questions.

Daily Notes: _____

JUDAH

June 6

Judah: one of the 12 tribes of Israel.

> **2 Chronicles 20:4** — *And Judah gathered themselves together, to ask help of the LORD: even out of all the cities of Judah they came to seek the LORD.*

Testimony

Wouldn't this be great to see in our nation today? Can you imagine an entire nation gathering to seek help from the Lord? They prayed for deliverance and later were given a promise of that deliverance. When you have a problem, who do you turn to for help? Be like Judah in this verse and seek your help from the Lord. Be careful who you choose to seek help from. Make sure you pray to the Lord about the situation. If you still want to talk to someone, pray to God about who that person should be. Do not follow your own wisdom, but seek instruction and help from the Lord. The Lord is the only One who promises deliverance and can give it.

Mission

When you need help, ask the Lord first before anyone else.

Daily Notes: _____

_____

_____

_____

_____

_____

_____

_____

JEHORAM

June 7

Jehoram: King of Judah for eight years in Jerusalem.

> **2 Chronicles 21:4** — *Now when Jehoram was risen up to the kingdom of his father, he strengthened himself, and slew all his brethren with the sword, and divers also of the princes of Israel.*

Testimony

Jehoram strengthened himself, which was his problem. He did not strengthen himself in the Lord or consult the Lord about how to rule a kingdom. In John 15:5 scripture tells us, "For without me ye can do nothing." Jehoram found out the hard way. He did wicked and evil things and did not serve the Lord. The result was a plague on the people and an incurable disease for himself. When Jehoram died, he wasn't buried in the sepulchers of the kings, even though he was a king.

Mission

Don't rely on your own strength. You will fail. Your flesh will fail. God never will!

Daily Notes: _____

_____

_____

_____

_____

_____

_____

_____

JERUSALEM

June 8

Jerusalem: a city in and the capital of Israel: an ancient holy city

> **2 Chronicles 20:27** — *Then they returned, every man of Judah and Jerusalem, and Jehoshaphat in the forefront of them, to go again to Jerusalem with joy; for the LORD had made them to rejoice over their enemies.*

Testimony

We were all born into sin. There comes a time in our lives when we reach the age of accountability — knowing right from wrong — when we must choose life or death; Heaven or Hell; Jesus or not? If you have accepted Christ as your Savior, keep that in the forefront of your mind. Ask the Lord to restore unto you the joy of your salvation. If you've accepted Christ, you have Jesus living inside of you. You can rejoice always, no matter what you face, because Jesus is working everything out for your good. The Lord caused them to rejoice over their enemies. How much more then should we be rejoicing over our enemies? How much more should we rejoice daily? Return to Jesus just like they went to Jerusalem. Ask Jesus to help you rejoice in every situation.

Mission

> **Philippians 4:4** — *Rejoice in the Lord always: and again I say, Rejoice.*

Daily Notes: _____

_____

_____

_____

_____

JOSHUA

June 9

Joshua: the successor of Moses as leader of the Israelites.

Deuteronomy 31:14 — *And the LORD said unto Moses, Behold, thy days approach that thou must die: Call Joshua, and present yourselves in the tabernacle of the congregation, that I may give him a charge. And Moses and Joshua went, and presented themselves in the tabernacle of the congregation.*

Testimony

The day we were born we started to die. We are getting older day by day; we're not growing younger. As the days approach, take you're calling seriously. Christ gave every one of us a call to tell others about Him. Make sure you appoint people in your life, and leave people in charge of spreading the gospel. Leave a legacy of Jesus to everyone that knew you. Let your goal be for them to say, "they loved Jesus." Make sure everyone close to you knows that the gospel of Jesus must be spread. Put people in charge and tell them that they must spread the gospel now. When you're gone, let somebody still be spreading the gospel because of your influence in his or her life.

Mission

Take charge.

Daily Notes: _____

_____

_____

_____

_____

JOINED

June 10

Joined: to bring in contact, connect, or bring or put together

> **2 Chronicles 18:1** — *Now Jehoshaphat had riches and honor in abundance, and joined affinity with Ahab.*

Testimony

Who are you joined with? We all need to be connected, completely joined and in tune with the Holy Spirit. Are you joined or connected with people who help or hinder your relationship with Christ? Are you hanging out with 'Jehoshaphats' who want to take everything to God in prayer, listen, and hear from the Lord? Or, are you hanging out with 'Ahabs' who just go and do, waiting on someone to point you in the right direction, even though you don't care. When Jehoshaphat sought the Lord, Ahab didn't like the evil outcome he was given. Don't join yourself with others that are completely out of God's will. Join yourself with those who will pray and help your relationship with the Lord, not hinder it.

Mission

Pray for God to send a 'Jehoshaphat' into your life. If you already have a person like Jehoshaphat, thank them for helping you in your walk with Christ.

Daily Notes: _____

_____

_____

_____

_____

JEHOZABAD

June 11

Jehozabad: A military leader under king Jehoshaphat

2 Chronicles 17:18 — *And next to him was Jehozabad, and with him a hundred and four score thousand ready prepared for the war.*

Testimony

There were several Jehozabads in the Bible. This particular man was known strictly as being a man of war for Jehoshaphat. Jehoshaphat had such a desire for serving God that he sent men around the kingdoms to teach the law of the Lord. The fear of the Lord fell upon the kingdoms and lands, and they made no war against Jehoshaphat. God will provide you what you need. He provided Jehoshaphat with thousands upon thousands of men ready to fight.

Don't you know that Jesus will fight your battles? Jesus will provide when there seems no way. He gave Jehoshaphat thousands and thousands of men; some who willingly offered themselves unto the Lord. Jesus knows what you need to face your battle and He will provide. Thousands and thousands is nothing compared to what our Jesus can do. Jehozabad isn't mentioned often, but can you imagine being known as being ready and prepared for war? Be prepared. Know who to get to fight your battles — that is Jesus.

Mission

Let Jesus fight your battles.

Daily Notes: _____

_____

_____

_____

JEHOVAH

Jehovah: God.

> **Genesis 1:3** — *And God said, Let there be light: and there was light.*

Testimony

God spoke and it was. God spoke and created everything. How powerful is that! All God has to do is speak. Let Jesus speak to you today. Only Jesus knows exactly what to say to speak to your heart.

Mission

Listen.

Daily Notes: _____

_____

_____

_____

_____

_____

_____

_____

_____

_____

_____

_____

_____

_____

JOSEPH

June 13

Joseph: the husband of Mary who was the mother of Jesus.

Matthew 1:20 — *But while he thought on these things, behold, the angel of the Lord appeared unto him in a dream, saying, Joseph, thou son of David, fear not to take unto thee Mary thy wife: for that which is conceived in her is of the Holy Ghost.*

Testimony

Joseph had a dream to convince him that Mary had conceived by the Holy Ghost. It wasn't an actual meeting or anything spectacular, but a dream — something that some of us do every night. Would a dream be enough to convince you of God's plan for your life? This shows us that God knows us. He knows how to speak to us and approach us in order for us to believe. For some of us, it might have taken something bigger than a dream to convince us of Mary carrying Jesus. However, when Jesus speaks to you, be obedient like Joseph. Once God confirms what He spoke, don't doubt, just do it!

Mission

Jesus will speak to you the way He knows how to reach you. Once He does, don't doubt.

Daily Notes: _____

_____

_____

_____

_____

_____

JAIL

Jail: a prison, especially for one awaiting trial or conviction.

> **Genesis 50:19** — *And Joseph said unto them, Fear not: for am I in the place of God?*

Testimony

Joseph spoke with his brothers and relieved their fears that he would surely hate them. Joseph's brothers were jealous of his relationship with their father and his coat of many colors. As a result of the coat, his brothers sold him into slavery. Joseph ended up falsely accused and thrown into the inner most parts of prison. At the end of his journey, Joseph ended up glorifying the Lord and being ruler over many. He told his brothers, "What you meant for evil, God meant for good." Joseph didn't dwell on his past or lose sight of serving the Lord. He served God and forgave his brothers. He actually comforted them and spoke kindly unto them.

What is your reaction when people treat you badly? Do you have a reaction such as Joseph did and glorify God in your situation? Joseph showed his brothers the love of Christ and made them fear God rather than man.

Mission

When people treat you badly, reply as Joseph did. Use it as a way to turn the situation around and give God glory. Your reward will be great.

Daily Notes: _____

_____

_____

_____

JAB

June 15

Jab: a poke with the end or point of something; a sharp, quick thrust.

> **Numbers 20:10** — *And Moses and Aaron gathered the congregation together before the rock, and he said unto them, Hear now, ye rebels; must we fetch you water out of this rock?*

Testimony

Moses took a jab at the rock instead of speaking to the rock like God had instructed. God told Moses in Exodus to strike the rock, but this time God told Moses to speak to the rock. Moses disobeyed God, and didn't get to enter into the land God had promised. Moses missed out on a blessing.

How many times have you chosen a jab of words, actions, or jokes instead of being obedient to the Lord? When we trust ourselves or give into our flesh, we're denying ourselves — and others — the blessings the Lord has for us. Jesus knows your heart and the heart of others. Jesus knows what you need to do better than you do.

Mission

Don't jab the rock when Jesus is telling you to speak to it.

Daily Notes: _____

_____

_____

_____

_____

_____

JAW

June 16

Jaw: forming the framework of the mouth.

> **Judges 15:15** — *And he found a new jawbone of an ass, and put forth his hand, and took it, and slew a thousand men therewith.*

> **Judges 15:19** — *But God clave an hollow place that was in the jaw, and there came water thereout; and when he had drunk, his spirit came again, and he revived: wherefore he called the name thereof En: hakkore, which is in Lehi unto this day.*

Testimony

Samson killed a thousand men with the jawbone of an ass. God delivered Samson twice with this jawbone — once to defeat his enemies, and again when he called upon the Lord for a drink. Out of the jawbone, a stream of water flowed under it. Samson drank and was revived.

This shows that when we call upon the Lord — whether it's to fight our battles or to revive us — the Lord answers our call. Our Savior is a loving, compassionate Savior who knows what we need. Use what Jesus sends to revive you. Samson picked up the jawbone and the Lord continued to bless him with it. Your answered prayers or your revival might not come in the way you're expecting, but it will come with what is best. Samson's came with a jawbone. What's yours? Don't overlook what Jesus is sending to revive you.

Mission

Be like Samson. Reach down and pick up your blessing.

Daily Notes: _____

_____

JAR

June 17

Jar: the quantity such a container can or does hold.

Matthew 26:7 — *There came unto him a woman having a alabaster box of very precious ointment, and poured it on his head, as he sat at meat.*

Testimony

Can you imagine being the man or the woman known as having the precious ointment? This woman made a choice. She could have just kept the jar for herself. She could have sold it or given it to the poor, which was suggested by the disciples. Instead, she put Jesus before anyone else and poured it over his head. She understood how precious Jesus is. She didn't view what was in her hands as merely a jar, but rather a precious ointment to be poured over her precious Savior.

Mission

Turn the "jars" in your life into precious ointments.

Daily Notes: _____

_____

_____

_____

_____

_____

_____

_____

_____

JOT

June 18

Jot: to write or mark down quickly or briefly

Daniel 5:5 — *In the same hour came forth the fingers of a man's hand, and wrote over against the candlestick upon the plaister of the wall of the kings palace: and the king saw the part of the hand that wrote:*

Testimony

When God jots something down, you had better pay attention. When God shows you a sign, you need to listen. When God writes with his finger upon a wall, take it as it is and obey. King Nebuchadnezzar and his son Belshazzar both had issues with pride. God changed Nebuchadnezzar into a beast of a field. He ate grass, grew feathers and claws. He was trapped in his new body. When he came out of his physical state, he said, "Now I praise and extol and honor the King of heaven, all whose works are truth and his ways judgment: and those that walk in pride he is able to abase."

Belshazzar knew what had happened to his father but, he had the "it won't happen to me" attitude. He repeated the mistakes his father made. That's when the writing on the wall occurred and interrupted Daniel. Again, Belshazzar had to deal with pride. He did not learn from his father and his mind was hardened with pride. Daniel reminded Belshazzar, which we all need daily reminders, that "God, in whose hand thy breath is, and whose are all thy ways, has thou not glorified." We need to remember to be humble and let go of our pride. It was important enough for God to remind both kings in supernatural ways to get rid of it.

Mission

Let go of your pride and be humble.

Daily Notes: _____

_____

JETHER

June 19

Jether: oldest of Gideon's seventy sons.

Judges 8:21 — *Then Zebah and Zalmunna said, Rise thou, and fall upon us: for as the man is, so is his strength. And Gideon arose, and slew Zebath and Zalmunna, and they took away the ornaments that were on their camel's necks.*

Testimony

Gideon was a brave warrior. His son was in the transitional stage and had not reached the status of a brave warrior yet. Gideon told Jether to slay Zebath and Zalmunna, but because of fear, Jether did not move. Gideon slayed them while they were making fun of his son. Gideon wanted his son to be a warrior, but he had to lead by example. You have to be the difference you want to see change in other people and the world.

Mission

Lead by example.

Daily Notes: _____

_____

_____

_____

_____

_____

_____

_____

_____

JERUBBAAL

June 20

Jerubbaal: Gideon

> **Judges 8:29** — *And Jerubbaal, the son of Joash went and dwelt in his own house.*

Testimony

Where does a person want to go to be able to relax completely? We want to come home and relax in our own house. Gideon fought and served the Lord, and won his battles with the help of the Lord. One of his victories was to dwell in Gideon's own house. The country was in quietness all the days of Gideon.

If you're unsettled, take comfort in Gideon's life. Let Jesus fight your battles. The end result will be peace. With Jesus you do not lose!

Mission

Dwell in peace and quietness with Jesus.

Daily Notes: _____

_____

_____

_____

_____

_____

_____

_____

_____

_____

JOTHAM

June 21

Jotham: Gideon's son

> **Judges 9:21** — *And Jotham ran away, and fled, and went to Beer, and dwelt there, for fear of Abimelech his brother.*

Testimony

Before Jotham ran and fled, he spoke a parable of curses that came to pass. He stood up for his father and pointed out that Abimelech was a poor choice for a king since he was not a man of God. The words Jotham spoke did come to pass, but he ran and hid instead of staying and encouraging himself in the Lord.

We are of no use to God when we continuously run and hide. We need to speak the truth of God in love, and stand up for what's right. Don't run and hide once you have spoken the truth. Let God use you.

Mission

Let life and blessings continuously flow out of your mouth rather than curses.

Daily Notes: _____

_____

_____

_____

_____

_____

_____

_____

_____

JACK

$$\mathscr{June}\ 22$$

Jack: a defensive coat.

> **1 Samuel 17:38** — *And David girded his sword upon his armor, and he assayed to go; for he had not proved it. And David said unto Saul, I cannot go with these; for I have not proved them. And David put them off him.*

Testimony

David went into battle without any defensive coat. He knew God had delivered him out of the hand of the lion's mouth and out of the paw of a bear. He knew who would also deliver him from Goliath. David said, "I come to thee in the name of the Lord of hosts, the God of the armies of Israel, whom thou has defied. This day the Lord deliver thee into mine hand; and I will smite thee, and take thine head from thee; and I will give the carcasses of the host of the Philistines this day unto the fowls of the air; that all the earth may know that there is a God in Israel."

David didn't go towards Goliath timidly. David went to defeat Goliath in the name of the Lord and did it boldly. He remembered that God had never let him down. He remembered that Jesus had always delivered him from trouble. He went boldly and defeated Goliath like he said he would, in the name of the Lord.

Mission

Don't forget who goes before you. So go boldly.

Daily Notes: _____

_____

_____

_____

_____

JONATHAN

June 23

Jonathan: son of Saul; friend of David.

1 Samuel 18:4 — *And Jonathan stripped himself of the robe that was upon him, and gave it to David, and his garments, even to his sword, and to his bow, and to his girdle.*

Testimony

Jonathan was the son of Saul and was the rightful heir to the throne. However, Jonathan was obedient to God's plan and knew that David was to be king. So Jonathan followed through with God's plan and did everything he could to assure that the throne would go to David. Jonathan could have got bitter, but instead he got better and went with God's plan instead of his own.

Mission

Don't get bitter; get better. Go with God's plan.

Daily Notes: _____

_____

_____

_____

_____

_____

_____

_____

_____

_____

JEALOUS

June 24

Jealous: feeling resentment because of another's success.

1 Samuel 18:30 — *Then the princes of the Philistines went forth: and it came to pass, after they went forth, that David behaved himself more wisely than all the servants of Saul; so that his name was much set by.*

Testimony

Despite Saul's jealous feelings towards David, David remained wiser than any of Saul's servants and Saul himself. David sought the Lord and the Lord provided ways in which David could escape the schemes of Saul. When given the chance to kill Saul, David chose not to. David knew Saul was one of the Lord's anointed. To kill him would be to go against the Lord. David was loyal to Saul, even though Saul was jealous and had tried to kill him several times.

You see an example of a jealous man — going against God's plan — and one that followed the Lord. Where do you find yourself from day to day? Are you being a "Saul" towards people, or are you being a "David" by obeying God and treating people the way Jesus would you want you to treat them?

Mission

Be a "David" towards people. Don't be jealous!

Daily Notes: _____

_____

_____

_____

_____

JERK

Jerk: to pull, twist, move, thrust, or throw with a quick, suddenly arrested motion:

> **1 Samuel 24:5-6** — *And it came to pass afterward, that David's heart smote him, because he had cut off Saul's skirt. And he said unto his men, The Lord forbid that I should do this thing unto my master, the Lords anointed, to stretch forth mine hand against him, seeing he is the anointed of the Lord.*

Testimony

When David jerked towards Saul to cut his skirt, instantly his heart smote him. Even though Saul had done David wrong several times, when it came time for David to have revenge, he couldn't kill him. He went ahead and cut his skirt even though his heart smote him. He felt remorse, convicted. He had done wrong. He told his men he had done wrong as well. He cried after Saul. His reaction caused Saul to admit his sin, and led Saul to acknowledge the Lord. Our reaction when people do us wrong can either lead people to the Lord or away from Him. Let your reaction, no matter what the circumstance is, lead people to the Lord.

Mission

React with the Lord in mind.

Daily Notes: _____

_____

_____

_____

_____

JESSE

June 26

Jesse: the father of David.

> **1 Samuel 25:10** — *And Nabal answered David's servants, and said, Who is David? And who is the son of Jesse? There be many servants now a days that break away every man from his master.*

Testimony

Nabal knew very well who the son of Jesse was. Nabal was a drunken man, and didn't care who he insulted. Are we not all God's children? Why do we pick and choose how we're going to react towards certain people? For example, if a person can help us in any way, we may treat them different than someone wanting something from us. Overall, that's not the right way to be. Nabel probably treated everyone around him the same way he treated David's servants. That wasn't good. Nabal wasn't capable of showing love.

We don't need to change who we are, how we act, or how we love depending on who we are talking to. We are all God's children. Jesus thought enough of us to die for everyone, so everyone deserves respect and love. Respect and love, with Christ in mind, will lead people to Jesus.

Mission

Treat everyone you meet the same. Show them respect, kindness, and love in Christ. That attitude will win people to Jesus. Anything else will make you look like Nabal.

Daily Notes: _____

_____

_____

JESHIMON

June 27

Jeshimon: "the waste" or "wilderness,"

1 Samuel 26:3 — *And Saul pitched in the hill of Hachilah, which is before Jeshimon, by the way. But David abode in the wilderness, and he saw that Saul came after him into the wilderness.*

Testimony

Both David and Saul were in the wilderness. David's spies found Saul lying in a trench asleep with his spear on the ground. David took Abishai with him to see Saul. Abishai wanted to see David kill Saul, but again, when given the chance, David served the Lord. As a result, Saul again admitted his sin.

No matter how many times you need to lay your sin down, Jesus will forgive each time. Saul repented many times. Don't think that you have messed up too big this time, or that you have gone too far. Run back to Jesus. He has taken that sin once and for all on the cross and it no longer belongs to you. Lay it down every time.

Mission

Don't pick it back up.

Daily Notes: _____

_____

_____

_____

_____

_____

_____

JUDGMENT

June 28

Judgment: determination.

1 Chronicles 10:13-14 — *So Saul died for his transgression which he committed against the Lord, even against the word of the LORD, which he kept not, and also for asking counsel of one that had a familiar spirit, to enquire of it; and enquired not of the Lord: therefore he slew him, and turned the kingdom over unto David the son of Jesse.*

Testimony

Saul's judgment from the Lord resulted in his continued disobedience to the Lord, as well as seeking advice from the witch of Endor rather than the Lord. Aren't you glad that we will not suffer judgement? Our judgement was paid for by the precious blood of Jesus Christ. Saul died because of his transgression against the Lord. Sin equals death. The precious blood of Jesus paid for our sins if you've accepted Him as your Savior. The price that was paid was high. Don't take sin lightly. Saul kept disobeying God and the result was death. Flee from your sin and into the arms of the One who paid for those sins. He set you free from all judgement, sin, and law.

Mission

Give your sins to the One who paid for them already — Jesus Christ. Stop running and trying to deal with your sins yourself. The price has been paid at a high cost. Accept what has already been paid for.

Daily Notes: _____

_____

_____

JEBUS

June 29

Jebus: an ancient Canaanite city taken by David: it later became Jerusalem.

> **1 Chronicles 11:5** — *And the inhabitants of Jebus said to David, Thou shalt not come hither. Nevertheless David took the castle of Zion, which is the city of David.*

Testimony

David was serving the Lord and knew he would rule over Israel. When the people of Jerusalem, known as the powerful Jebusites, said to David, "Don't come," David just went. He didn't listen to what others said. Instead, David focused on God's promises and had the Jebusites killed. David knew the Lord was with him. Don't let anything stop you from God's plan for your life. The only one that can stop it is you. Don't listen to negativity or anything that is untrue. Stick with the truth and with what lines up with the Word of God.

Mission

Nevertheless, hold on to God's promises.

Daily Notes: _____

_____

_____

_____

_____

_____

_____

JUNE

Reflection of the month of June:

Hebrews 11:33-34 — *Who, through faith, subdued kingdoms, wrought righteousness, obtained promises, stopped the mouth of lions, quenched the violence of fire, escaped the edge of the sword, out of weakness were made strong, waxed valiant in fight, turned to fight the armies of the aliens.*

Testimony
These are just a few things that the faithful servants of the Bible did for the Lord. True faith holds on to the very end. I encourage you to hold on and to not give up. Remember that your weakness is made strong through Christ. When you are weak, He is strong.

Mission
Reflect on the times when you were weak, but Christ was strong. How did the situation go when Christ was in control? Reflect on this and tell others. It's part of your testimony.

Daily Notes: _____

_____

_____

_____

_____

_____

_____

_____

_____

JASHOBEAM

July 1

Jasobeam: one of David's chief heroes who joined him at Ziklag.

1 Chronicles 11:11 — *And this is the number of the mighty men whom David had; Jashobeam, a Hachmonite, the chief of the captains: he lifted up his spear against three hundred slain by him at one time.*

Testimony

David needed mighty men to defeat the Philistines the Lord gave him mighty men. The Lord will give you what you need so His will can be accomplished for your life. Don't miss the people, places, and things that Jesus is putting in your life to help you accomplish His will. The opportunities Jesus is giving you will help you to glorify Him. Jesus sent David mighty men, and one of those men killed three hundred at one time. What Jesus gives us is better than anything we could try to get on our own.

Mission

Look around and thank the Lord for giving you what you need to receive His promises, plans, and provision for your life.

Daily Notes: _____

_____

_____

_____

_____

_____

_____

_____

JOHANAN

July 2

Johanan: One of the Gadite heroes who joined David

1 Chronicles 12:8 — *And of the Gadites there separated themselves unto David into the hold of the wilderness of men of might, and men of war fit for the battle, that could handle shield and buckler, whose face were like the faces of lions, and were as swift as the roes upon the mountains;*

Testimony

Johanan was among some of the Gadites who joined David for battle. Can you imagine being known in the Bible as a man of might, war, fit for battle, able to handle shield and buckler whose face was like a lion, and swift as roes on the mountains? As Christians, we need lost people to look at us and see the same — that our hope, strength, and fight lies in Jesus. People need to look at us and see that we are Christians — fit for battle and prepared for anything because we have Jesus Christ. Jesus will prepare you to be fit for battle. Don't depend on your own strength. Your own strength is never enough to fight the devil.

Mission

How do you prepare for anything you will face in life? Don't forget that there is power in the name of Jesus.

Daily Notes: _____

_____

_____

_____

_____

_____

JEHIAH

July 3

Jehiah: doorkeeper for the ark

1 Chronicles 15:24 — *And Shebaniah, and Jehoshaphat, and Nethaneel, and Amasai, and Zechariah, and Benaiah, and Eliezer, the priests, did blow with the trumpets before the ark of God: and Obed-edom and Jehiah were doorkeepers for the ark.*

Testimony

To move the ark of God, it took many people playing many different roles. This sounds like our churches today. No matter what role you play, you are important in the body of Christ. Just your presence alone can lift someone up in the congregation that you know nothing about. Maybe you're a doorkeeper, like Jehiah. You are still needed. Jesus needs you to do your role and be a part of the body of Christ. No role is too big or too small. Each role is important. The body can't function well with a broken limb. That's how the body of Christ *limps* when you are not at church. Jesus said, "Don't forsake the assembling of ourselves together." (Hebrews 10:25) We should model Jesus' role and do what He did. He went to the temple. You might think, "I don't have a role!" Well, pray for Jesus to show you the role he wants you to be a part of. You might already be a role model for someone else and you have no idea.

Mission

Trust Jesus and seek out the role he wants you to have in the body of Christ. If you want to grow in the Lord, ask him to give you a role in your church and community.

Daily Notes: _____

_____

JUMPY

July 4

Jumpy: subject to sudden, involuntary starts, especially from nervousness, fear.

> **Numbers 14:9** — *Only rebel not ye against the LORD, neither fear ye the people of their land; for they are bread for us: their defense is departed from them, and the LORD is with us: fear them not.*

Testimony

Only Joshua, Caleb and their families got to enter the Promised Land. The rest of the children of Israel feared and doubted God. They showed no faith so they did not get to enter into the Promised Land. They were fearful and nervous instead of having faith. Joshua and Caleb didn't look at the giants or the walls; instead they had hope in the Lord and faith in His promises. The Lord had delivered them and He would do it again. They tried to urge the children of Israel to believe and not fear, however, because they didn't have hope in the Lord, they didn't get to see the promise. No matter what the circumstances look like or what people are saying about the circumstances, hold on to God's promises and the fact that He is faithful. God will not fail you.

I was driving to work one morning, praying about a situation. "Lord, help me to not be stressed," I prayed. The Lord replied, "I wouldn't have blessed you with it to create stress in you." Stress is not of the Lord. Don't focus on the stress. You don't want to miss out on the blessing, like the children of Israel did.

Mission

Find hope in Jesus and hang on to the promise no matter what! Don't be jumpy about it. He wants to bless you, not stress you. Think on this fact all day, "You are blessed, not stressed."

Daily Notes: _____

JEREMIAH

Jeremiah: a major prophet.

> **Jeremiah 3:22** — *Return, ye backsliding children, and I will heal your backslidings. Behold, we come unto thee; for thou art the Lord our God.*

Testimony

Backsliding means to *turn back* or *turn away from*. It could also be a failure to grow spiritually in the Lord. We need to deny our flesh daily and be about the Lord's business, doing things the way Jesus would want us to verses doing things our own way or in our own understanding. We should always desire to follow the Lord's path for our lives and grow in grace so that we won't back slide. Turn away from sin and run to Jesus.

Jeremiah had such a love for people that he preached for forty years. He shows us throughout scripture that we need to "speak the truth in love." His message is clear: *return to the Lord and do not black slide anymore*. Instead, fall forward, growing in the grace and knowledge of the Lord.

Mission

Grow.

Daily Notes: _____

_____

_____

_____

_____

_____

_____

JEPHUNNEH

July 6

Jephunneh: The father of Caleb, who was Joshua's companion in exploring Canaan.

> **Joshua 14:6** — *Then the children of Judah came unto Joshua of Gilgad: and Caleb the son of Jephunneh the Kenezite, said unto him, Thou knowest the thing that the Lord said unto Moses the man of God concerning me and thee in Kadeshbarnea.*

Testimony

Joshua and Caleb knew what God had told them. They knew God said they could have the land. Out of the 12 spies, Joshua and Caleb were the only ones who remembered, "the thing the Lord had said unto Moses." Remember what the Lord has told you. Despite all the chatter from satan and the world, hold on to what Jesus has told you. Maybe Jesus has spoken to you personally and told you, "I am with you" or "I will take care of this." Or maybe you have found hope and comfort in the Word. Whatever the case may be, don't forget to hold on to "the thing" and remember what the Lord has told you. It will come to pass.

Mission

Don't forget!

Daily Notes: _____

_____

_____

_____

_____

_____

JERICHO

July 7

Jericho: strongest fortress in all the land of Canaan.

> **Joshua 6:2** — *And the Lord said unto Joshua, See, I have given into thine hand Jericho, and the king thereof, and the mighty men of valour.*

Testimony

Joshua's battle was strange in the eyes of men, but God had the perfect plan. No matter how odd it may seem, if God's telling you to do something, do it! God's wisdom and thoughts are high above ours.

God sees the whole picture while we're only capable of seeing what's right in front of us. God knew the best way to win the battle for Joshua. All he had to do was trust and obey. Jesus delivered Joshua and gave him Jericho because of his obedience. His battle strategy was unique because it was God's plan. The people marched around the city walls for seven days then the walls fell down. No matter what God's telling you to do, don't stop until you finish. If they had stopped on day three or four, the walls wouldn't have fallen down. They had to listen to God and push on until day seven and then they saw God's deliverance.

Mission

Don't stop short. Push on and see God's plan come to pass.

Daily Notes: _____

_____

_____

_____

_____

JOIN

Join: to bring in contact, connect, or bring or put together:

Matthew 19:6 — *Wherefore they are no more twain, but one flesh. What therefore God hath joined together, let not man put asunder.*

Testimony

When you enter into marriage, it is a unity with God, and you become one flesh with your husband or wife. Not only have you made vows to each other, but you have also made a promise to God. Christ gives us examples and teaches us through His word how to treat one another and how to love one another. He also gives us examples from His Word of what to do when times get tough. God never breaks His promise to you, so do you best to not break the unity of one flesh with Christ in your marriage. Ecclesiastes 4:12 says, "And if one prevail against him, two shall withstand and a threefold cord is not quickly broken." With Christ as the center of your marriage, it will not fail. You might be thinking, "Well, you have no idea what my situation is." You're right, I don't, but Jesus does and He has exactly what you need. Just give it to Him.

Mission

Remember the promise you made to Jesus. Do your best to honor the Lord and be the husband or wife Christ wants you to be. Make sure your marriage or relationships line up with what the Word of God says.

Daily Notes: _____

_____

_____

_____

JOYFUL

July 9

Joyful: full of joy

> **Isaiah 51:11** — *Therefore the redeemed of the LORD shall return, and come with singing unto Zion; and everlasting joy shall be upon their head: they shall obtain gladness and joy; and sorrow and morning shall flee away.*

Testimony

God does not want us to experience temporary joy. He wants us to be consumed with joy. God wants us completely full of joy, overflowing with gladness. When Jesus gives us joy, it lasts. It completely takes away all mourning and sorrow. Jesus will give us joy unspeakable that is full of glory! Jesus gives us everlasting joy, meaning it lasts and never runs out.

Mission

Find joy in the Lord.

Daily Notes: _____

_____

_____

_____

_____

_____

_____

_____

_____

_____

_____

JEEP

July 10

Jeep: a small, rugged military motor vehicle having four-wheel drive

> **Matthew 6:8** — *Be not ye therefore like unto them: for your Father knoweth what things ye have need of, before ye ask him.*

Testimony

Most of us know what a jeep is or what they look like. Some of you live in the country, like I do. Lots of times we use our jeep for seeing the beautiful countryside or going through the mud. My cousin came in from the city and I thought I would show her around. We were in the middle of the woods when the jeep broke down. All I knew to do was pray. The jeep started right back up. Years later she mentioned it. It was something that stuck in both of our minds forever. We can take comfort in the fact that all we have to do is *ask*. Jesus knows what we have need of before we even pray. He knows our minds and what's in our hearts. He knows our heart's truest desires. Our desire that day was to get on the road and keep going. Jesus answered that prayer. He is faithful.

When I moved into my first home, my dad helped me move in my washer and dryer, only to find out that one of them wasn't working. We looked around and couldn't figure it out, so I laid hands on it and prayed and it started to work. When someone asked my dad how we got it working, he said, "Kayla prayed."

Why do we make things complicated? Jesus makes things simple. He already knows what we need before we pray, so why delay praying? We try to figure out how to fix it, but when we couldn't, we prayed. Pray first and save yourself some time, worry, and hassle. Jesus not only has the answer, He *is* the answer.

Mission

Take everything to the Lord in prayer. He answers every time.

Daily Notes: _____

JEWELS

July 11

Jewels: a precious possession.

> **Matthew 6:21** — *For where your treasure is, there will your heart be also.*

Testimony

Earthly gain is temporary. Your faithfulness and obedience to the Lord are treasures in Heaven forever. Your heart condition determines where your treasures lie. Jesus knows our hearts and our true motives for everything we do. Make sure your heart isn't drawn to the accumulation of your material things. Instead, make sure you're more concerned with Heavenly gain and the rewards for faithful service to Jesus. Give attention to what He is calling you to do, rather than gathering an abundance of earthly jewels.

Mission

Pray for Jesus to give you a heart examination. Pray for your treasures and motives to be Christ-centered and Heaven-bound.

Daily Notes: _____

_____

_____

_____

_____

_____

_____

_____

_____

_____

JAKAN

July 12

Jakan: one of the sons of Ezer, the son of Seir the Horite

1 Chronicles 1:42 — *The sons of Ezer; Bilha, and Zaven, and Jakan. The sons of Dishan; Uz, and Aran.*

Testimony

Can you imagine your name being important enough to be noted in the Bible? Jakan was one of several names mentioned in the genealogical lists at the beginning of 1 Chronicles. Can you imagine being among the list of names of the righteous individuals who lived before the flood, from the line being traced from Noah's sons to Abraham? Because of Abraham's obedience, generations after him are still seeing the blessings and promises from the Lord. You can contribute to the generational blessings for your family. You can also break generational curses. Pray and give your family to Jesus. Make sure when you leave this world, your obedient life, the prayers you've prayed and the curses you broke off your family through Jesus Christ, is the legacy you leave behind for them.

Mission

Let Jesus be seen in your life. Pray prayers of blessings on your family now and for generations to come.

Daily Notes: _____

_____

_____

_____

_____

_____

_____

JOINING

July 13

Joining: to come into the company of; meet or accompany:

Exodus 11:29 — *And Moses said, Thou hast spoken well, I will see thy face again no more.*

Testimony

Think about the weight this verse carries. It carries eternal weight. Jesus calls you to spread the gospel. Pharaoh's heart was hardened. He would not let God's people go. Don't let your heart get hardened for continuously wanting to see souls saved to Jesus. Think about that verse: "I will see thy face again no more." How many faces that we see now, will we not see again? How many faces that we see now, will we see again? As a born-again Christian, God commands us to spread the gospel. Keep that reality in the front of your mind. Let this verse be a reminder that we want to see people — and our loved ones — again. Tell everybody you know about Jesus.

Mission

Give people a chance to join Jesus.

Daily Notes: _____

_____

_____

_____

_____

_____

_____

JOINT-HEIRS

July 14

Joint-Heirs: a connection; made right to an inheritance.

Romans 8:17 — *And if children, then heirs; heirs of God, and joint-heirs with Christ; if so be that we suffer with him, that we may be also glorified together.*

Testimony

My grandmother used to sing an old hymn that said, "We have a mansion just over the hill top." When we accept Christ, we receive His spirit inside of us. He then calls us to be joint-heirs. We have a right, because of the price Jesus paid on the cross, to an inheritance in Heaven. That mansion my grandmother used to sing about is waiting for the children of God, but is it an inheritance just for eternal life? No, it is an inheritance now! We have been joined with Christ. He lives inside of us. The inheritance begins now with all of Christ's blessings and promises given to us.

Be fully devoted to Christ, making that connect with Jesus. Listen to Him daily. The same power that raised Jesus from the dead lives inside of you. If you're not experiencing your inheritance now, it's because you're spending too much time in this world.

Mission

Separate yourself and see what Jesus wants to give you. It's better than anything this world can give. You are a joint-heir because of Jesus.

Daily Notes: _____

_____

_____

_____

JAIL

July 15

Jail: a prison, especially one for the detention of persons awaiting trial or convicted of minor offenses.

2 Timothy 1:8 — *Be not thou therefore ashamed of the testimony of our Lord, nor of me his prisoner: but be thou partakers of the afflictions of the gospel according to the power of God.*

Testimony

Paul was in jail; yet he was so in tune and in touch with Jesus that he knew he was in the direct will of God. Paul knew he was only in prison because that's where Jesus wanted him to be. He was only in Rome because that's where Jesus wanted him to be. Even if your circumstances are like Paul's, be content just knowing that Jesus is everywhere with you.

Mission

Be content.

Daily Notes: _____

_____

_____

_____

_____

_____

_____

_____

_____

JANNES

July 16

Jannes: one of the Egyptians who "withstood Moses"

> **2 Timothy 3:7** — *Ever learning, and never able to come to the knowledge of the truth.*

Testimony

Jannes stood against Moses. Jannes didn't believe the truth. Jannes didn't believe God's miracles. Was there a time in your life when you stood with Jannes? Was there a time in your life when you stood with Moses? Moses proclaimed the truth and stood fast on the knowledge of Christ and trusted in Jesus' miracles.

No matter where you stood before, make sure you're standing on the truth now. We could all say at different points in our lives that we stood with Jannes' doubting. And there are times we have stood with Moses' proclaiming. Now that you know the truth and have the knowledge of Jesus Christ, never stand like 'Jannes' again.

Mission

Believe and let your actions show that there is no truth apart from God's Word.

Daily Notes: _____

_____

_____

_____

_____

_____

_____

_____

_____

JAMBRES

July 17

Jambres: one of those who opposed Moses in Egypt

2 Timothy 3:8 — *Now as Jannes and Jambres withstood Moses, so do these also resist the truth: men of corrupt minds, reprobate concerning the faith.*

Testimony
People like Jannes and Jambres exist in our lives today. How did Moses deal with it? He *didn't* deal with it; he didn't have to. The Lord delivered him! The Lord delivered Moses so he kept preaching the Word and spreading the gospel. Moses acted on what he learned because he knew that all scripture was inspired by God and always leads to righteousness. He stood on the Word and Jesus defended him.

Mission
Stand.

Daily Notes: _____

_____

_____

_____

_____

_____

_____

_____

_____

_____

JUSTLY

July 18

Justly: in a just manner; honestly; fairly

2 Timothy 4:3 — *For the time will come when they will not endure sound doctrine; but after their own lusts shall they heap to themselves teachers, having itchy ears.*

Testimony

When you preach the Word, or when you tell others about Christ, do it in a justly manner. Teachers who appeal to itchy ears tell people what they *want* to hear, not what they *need* to hear. Do the work of the Lord and tell the truth in love. Telling someone what they want to hear and going against the Word of God will lead to destruction. Show your love towards Christ and people. Spread the word justly.

Mission

Tell the truth.

Daily Notes: _____

_____

_____

_____

_____

_____

_____

_____

_____

_____

JUDGE

July 19

Judge: a person qualified to pass a critical judgment

> **Romans 3:10** — *As it is written, There is none righteous, no, not one:*

Testimony

Since none of us are righteous on our own, how can we judge one another? Jesus is our only judge because He is the only one who makes us righteous. It was nothing we did. It was nothing we deserved. If you have accepted Christ as your Savior, His blood washed away all your sins and made you righteous. Since you did nothing to earn it, how can you judge it?

Mission

Accept righteousness through Christ, then freely give it rather than judge whose worthy of it.

Daily Notes: _____

_____

_____

_____

_____

_____

_____

_____

_____

_____

JOLT

July 20

Jolt: to bring to a desired state sharply or abruptly:

> **Ecclesiastes 3:1** — *To every thing there is a season, and a time to every purpose under the heaven:*

Testimony

Solomon reminds us that life brings us a lot of ups and downs and we will go through different emotions along the way. However, God is sovereign and is in the background of all life's events. Let the opportunity to make time for God give you a jolt to spur you into action. Jesus has a blessing He wants you to receive. It's up to you to get into a place to receive it. He wants you to jolt!

Mission

Jolt.

Daily Notes: _____

_____

_____

_____

_____

_____

_____

_____

_____

_____

_____

JAM

July 21

Jam: spreadable substance containing fruit.

Jude 1:1 — *Jude, the servant of Jesus Christ, and brother of James, to them that are sanctified by God the Father, and preserved in Jesus Christ, and called.*

Testimony

People who accept Christ as their personal Savior are sanctified and preserved by Jesus. That alone should get you yelling with excitement right now! You are *kept* for Jesus Christ! *Preserved* makes me think of jam. My grandmother would preserve strawberries and make jam. Part of the canning process was sealing the jars which kept the contents good until you opened it. She preserved it until later. Jesus has set you apart for a good purpose. You are *kept* in His embrace. Even if the world tries to open you, you were set apart only for Jesus Christ and His return.

Mission

Believe you have been set apart.

Daily Notes: _____

_____

_____

_____

_____

_____

_____

_____

_____

JAMES

July 22

James: a book of the New Testament

James 1:17 — *Every good gift and every perfect gift is from above, and cometh down from the Father of lights, with whom is no variableness, neither shadow of turning.*

Testimony

One day I was in my kitchen praying and I said, "Lord, how do I know it's You telling me to do something and not satan or myself?" The Lord answered and said, "If it's good, it's me." It's truly that simple. If it's good, it's Jesus. If it's not good, it's something you want nothing to do with. Every good and perfect gift is from Jesus.

Mission

Thank Jesus today!

Daily Notes: _____

_____

_____

_____

_____

_____

_____

_____

_____

_____

_____

_____

JITTERY

July 23

Jittery: extremely tense and nervous; jumpy:

Acts 12:14 — *And when she knew Peters voice, she opened not the gate for gladness, but ran in, and told how Peter stood before the gate.*

Testimony

The woman that opened the door was Rhoda. Peter was in prison and everyone was praying for him. There was a knock at the door and Rhoda knew it was Peter's voice without even opening the door. She ran and told the others he was there. Their prayers were answered. They called her crazy! Rhoda probably got discouraged real quick. I could imagine her defending herself or possibly being a little offended at being called 'crazy.' Aren't we like that sometimes? Our prayers are answered! We have to have the faith to believe that! When Jesus answers our prayers, why do we still doubt? Are we calling ourselves crazy? Don't doubt that Jesus answers all of your prayers according to His will!

Mission

Your prayers will be answered. Don't think it's crazy. It's truth!

Daily Notes: _____

_____

_____

_____

_____

_____

JUNEBUG

July 24

Junebug: beetles that are common in late spring

Acts 12:13 — *And as Peter knocked at the door of the gate, a damsel came to hearken, named Rhoda.*

Testimony

A damsel — a servant — has her little part in our world just like the Junebug has its little part in our big world. Do you think any part or any creature or creation is too small to God? We might view Rhoda's part as small, but she had a big part in the world where she was a servant. Jesus knew Rhoda's heart and there is no such thing as a small part with Jesus. So if you feel your part is small, like Rhoda, know that Jesus views all parts as equally important and you are needed. Jesus is big enough to be anywhere, yet small enough to fit into our hearts.

Mission

Jesus needs you!

Daily Notes: _____

_____

_____

_____

_____

_____

_____

_____

_____

JAH

July 25

Jah: 1530s, a form of Hebrew Yah, short for Yahweh "Jehovah

Exodus 6:3 — *And I appeared unto Abraham, unto Isaac, and unto Jacob, by the name of God Almighty, but by my name JEHOVAH was I not known to them.*

Testimony

Why would God appear unto them in a name they didn't know? God was about to manifest His name to them. They may not have realized the full meaning of God's name yet, but they were about to experience the meaning of God being Almighty. God is revealing Himself through His actions, which is what *Yahweh* means. Realize that Jesus' presence in your life is powerful. If you're not experiencing it, then call upon Yahweh Jesus to fill you with His power and might. Pray that Jesus will be ever so real in your life and that His powerful hand would be present — recognized, not only by you, but by everyone around you.

The people would not listen to Moses so God gave him instructions for the people. God's power brought plague after plague after plague. Some might view the plagues as awful [and they certainly were], but another way to look at it is how much God loved His people. God wanted Pharaoh to let the people go. Whatever you're going through, know that God can deliver you through it. He is all-powerful.

Mission

Yahweh will meet your needs.

Daily Notes: _____

_____

_____

JEHOVAH-SHALOM

Jehovah-Shalom: Jehovah send peace, the name which Gideon gave to the altar he erected on the spot at Ophrah where the angel appeared to him

> **Judges 6:24** — *Then Gideon built an altar there unto the Lord, and called it Jehovah-shalom: unto this day it is yet in Ophrah of the Abiezrites.*

Testimony

Gideon built an altar unto the Lord; the name meant peace. Isn't that what Jesus is to us? He is my peace! *Unto this day it is there.* How many people see that altar in a lifetime? What are we doing to make an eternal effect like Gideon? The Bible says, "Unto this day"...that's forever! Let's make an eternal effect like Gideon and make sure that people know that what we are doing is for Jesus.

Mission

Do it this day!

Daily Notes: _____

_____

_____

_____

_____

_____

_____

_____

JUDGES

Judges: a book in the Old Testament

> **Judges 1:1** — *Now after the death of Joshua it came to pass, that the children of Israel asked the Lord, saying, Who shall go up for us against the Canaanites first, to fight against them?*

Testimony

The Lord replied unto them, "Judah shall go up. I have delivered the land into his hand." When I read this verse I got a little annoyed with the Children of Israel. I was thinking: "When are they going to learn who fights for them?" Aren't you glad that we don't have to find anyone to fight for us because Jesus will?

We can all relate to the children of Israel. We have found ourselves searching for ways to win our battles. Jesus already has what we need to become overcomers. Look no further than Jesus. He has what you need to win your battle.

Mission

Face your battles with the truth that "Jesus wins!"

Daily Notes: _____

_____

_____

_____

_____

_____

_____

_____

_____

JEHOIAKIM

July 28

Jehoiakim: he whom Jehovah has set up, the second son of Josiah, and eighteenth king of Judah, which he ruled over for eleven years

> **Jeremiah 22:18** — *Therefore thus saith the Lord concerning Jehoiakim the son of Josiah king of Judah; they shall not lament for him, saying, Ah my brother! Or, Ah sister! They shall not lament for him, saying, Ah lord! Or, Ah his glory!*

Testimony

God warned Jehoiakim about his disobedience. Jehoiakim didn't listen. He still made his house unrighteous. He used his neighbor's service without wages. He was unjust and he wanted everything for himself. He shed innocent blood.

God loves us enough to warn us of our disobedience. If we continue down disobedience's path, we will not only suffer worldly consequences, but even worse, eternal consequences. Jehoiakim's result was the Lord saying, "Bury him with the donkeys and cast him out of the gates of Jerusalem." Don't take the warnings God is giving you lightly. Turn your life around to where you're walking towards Jesus.

Mission

Turn around.

Daily Notes: _____

_____

_____

_____

_____

_____

JEHOVAH JIREH

July 29

Jehovah Jireh: God sees, or God will provide

Genesis 22:14 — *And Abraham called the name of that place Jehovah-Jireh: as it is said to this day, In the mount of the Lord it shall be seen.*

Testimony

Abraham was called by God to sacrifice his son, Isaac. We have to understand that God never tempts us with evil, but He will test our faith at times. God knew the outcome of the test. That was the only reason God would test Abraham with his future, God sees our future and knows the outcome as well. Abraham knew God and knew He was faithful. Abraham spoke life and comforted his son, Isaac. He said, "God will provide a lamb." At the last moment Abraham looked and saw a ram caught in a thicket. The Lord provided.

Abraham then built an altar and called it *Jehovah Jireh.* Abraham had faith that God would provide.

Mission

Know who your provider is.

Daily Notes: _____

_____

_____

_____

_____

_____

_____

_____

JEHOVAH SHAMMAH

Jehovah Shammah: the Lord is there

>**Ezekiel 48:35** — *It was round about eighteen thousand measures: and the name of the city that day shall be, the Lord is there.*

Testimony

The Lord is there. Wherever you are, the Lord is there! Wherever you go, the Lord is there! Tomorrow don't fear, because the Lord is there! Today don't fear, because the Lord is there! Whatever you're doing or wherever you're going, take comfort in the fact that the Lord is there!

Mission

Let someone else know that the Lord is there!

Daily Notes: _____

_____

_____

_____

_____

_____

_____

_____

_____

_____

_____

JULY

Reflection of the month of July:

John 12:46 — *I am come a light into the world, that whosoever believeth on me should not abide in darkness.*

Testimony

If you are a Christian, darkness doesn't exist for you. I don't know about you, but knowing that Jesus is my light, the light of the world, and that in Him is no darkness at all, brightens me up. I have Jesus living inside of me and if you have accepted Him, so do you. Because of this, we are the light of the world.

Show the light that Jesus gave you to the world. Just a little bit of light can illuminate a whole lot of darkness.

Mission

Let your light shine bright. This month reflect on how your light shines. Next month make sure it shines even brighter.

Daily Notes: _____

_____

_____

_____

_____

_____

_____

_____

_____

_____

ACTUALITY

August 1

Actuality: actual existence; reality

Revelation 22:13 — *I am Alpha and Omega, the beginning and the end, the first and the last.*

Testimony

The actuality of our lives is: Jesus is real; Jesus is everywhere; and if you have accepted Him, then Jesus' Spirit lives inside of you. He is the beginning and the end — the first and the last and everything in between. We need to keep this reality in the forefront of our minds. If this is a reality in our lives, we will see Jesus in every aspect of our life. If I keep the reality that Jesus is real and is coming back in my mind at all times, how much more effective will I be at spreading the gospel? How much more effective will I be at letting people know Jesus loves them? This is our reality and we need to keep reminding ourselves of our reality every day. Don't let anyone tell you the reality of your situation. The reality from beginning to end is Jesus.

Mission

Get excited! Your reality is Jesus!

Daily Notes: _____

_____

_____

_____

_____

_____

_____

AWARE

August 2

Aware: informed; alert

> **Luke 6:25** — *Woe unto you that are full! For ye shall hunger. Woe unto that laugh now! For ye shall mourn and weep.*

Testimony

Laughing is a good thing when done with a good, cheerful heart. The laughing in this scripture is talking about the misfortune of others. Whether it's laughing out loud or in our hearts, Jesus knows, so this is something we need to be aware of. Jesus is telling us how to treat others. Be aware that Jesus is with you all the time. We are all His children.

Mission

Never laugh at the misfortune of God's children.

Daily Notes: _____

_____

_____

_____

_____

_____

_____

_____

_____

_____

_____

ALL

August 3

All: the whole of

> **Isaiah 1:18** — *Come now, and let us reason together, saith the Lord: though your sins be as scarlet, they shall be as white as snow; though they be red like crimson, they shall be as wool.*

Testimony

Jesus stands ready to forgive all men of all sin. Let him! Understand that what Jesus did is for all men, and it covers all of your life from beginning to end. When you accept Christ, He washes your sins white as snow. Get over the guilt of your past or decisions you have made. Turn your life over to Jesus and start living. Don't take what Jesus did lightly. Instead, let what He did cover all of your life.

Mission

Accept Jesus and be covered in all of His unchanging grace.

Daily Notes: _____

_____

_____

_____

_____

_____

_____

_____

_____

ABRAHAM

August 4

Abraham: name meaning "father of many." Father of Isaac.

Genesis 22:8 — *And Abraham said, My son, God will provide himself a lamb for a burnt offering: so they went both of them together.*

Testimony

Isaac was to be offered as a sacrifice; but Abraham had faith and knew God would provide a substitute offering. He spoke life and comforted his son by telling him God would provide. God provided a ram. God always provides something greater than we could ever imagine.

Mission

Trust Jesus. He never stops providing and it's always greater than we could ever imagine.

Daily Notes: _____

_____

_____

_____

_____

_____

_____

_____

_____

_____

ADMIRATION

August 5

Admiration: worthy of appreciation or respect

> **Colossians 4:5** — *Walk in wisdom toward them that are without, redeeming the time.*

Testimony

When my husband and I were dating, I saw a letter on his dresser. I never knew who actually wrote it to him. Deep down I always felt like it was my pastor's wife, caring for him while he was out of church. I asked her about it one day and she just said, "probably." We need to redeem the time. Not only for those who are lost, but also for those who have taken a break from coming to church. While he wasn't strongly serving the Lord at the time, the letter still meant enough that it was displayed on his dresser. If you notice a person without Jesus or who has stepped away from the Lord, take an opportunity to help in bringing them back. Create a way of showing them you care. Do it so often that when someone asks you, "was that you?" you can just turn around and say "probably."

Mission

Show admiration towards each other.

Daily Notes: _____

_____

_____

_____

_____

_____

_____

APPARENTLY

August 6

Apparently: as far as one knows or can see

> **Ruth 2:3** — *And she went, and came, and gleaned in the field after the reapers: and her hap was to light on a part of the field belonging unto Boaz, who was of the kindred of Elimelech.*

Testimony

Apparently, Ruth ended up in the field that was owned by Boaz. Looking at this situation through carnal vision, it might look like this was a coincidence. But looking at this plan through spiritual eyes, we can see that this was the will of God and it didn't happen by chance. Ruth ended up being in the field that blessed her, changed her whole life through a marriage that brought life and put her in line to Jesus Christ. You aren't where you are in this life for no reason. Get your eyes fixed on Jesus and have Him show you why you are where you are in life. Whether it is your job, location, friendship, or marriage, Jesus is faithful and will show you what He wants you to do. Jesus won't leave you. He will show you the way.

Mission

Look for the blessing in where you are.

Daily Notes: _____

_____

_____

_____

_____

_____

AGNOSTIC

August 7

Agnostic: a person who holds that the existence of the ultimate cause, as God, and the essential nature of things are unknowledgeable, a non-believer.

> **Ecclesiastes 3:1** — *To every thing there is a season, and a time to every purpose under the heaven:*

Testimony

We all know, or know of a person who claims to be agnostic. This doesn't surprise Jesus. There have been people throughout time who didn't believe in Him. That doesn't mean that Jesus doesn't love them, or won't call them. He can send people into their paths to point them towards Himself. Their time will come. There is a purpose for their lives and their season will come when the Lord reveals that. Encourage these nonbelievers. Pray for opportunities, seek chances, and pray, "Jesus, open their eyes so they won't deny you anymore and will have a personal relationship with you." Jesus never fails.

Mission

You might be the person that Jesus put in their life to lead them towards Him. Make the most of every opportunity to lead someone to the Lord. Pray this bold prayer for them, "Whatever it takes Lord, whatever it takes. Whatever it takes for them to believe in you."

Daily Notes: _____

_____

_____

_____

_____

ANSWER

August 8

Answer: a spoken or written reply or response to a question, request, or letter.

> **Ruth 3:18** — *Then said she, Sit still, my daughter, until thou know how the matter will fall: for the man will not be in rest, until he have finished the thing this day.*

Testimony

Ruth had to wait for the answer. How will Boaz, the man she's trying to impress, react? Have you ever had to wait for an answer? It could be anything in life. I was thinking about some major life decisions: where to move, what house to buy, what church to go to. At one point in my life the Lord gave me peace by saying, "Instead of looking *for* the answer, look *to* the answer." Jesus is the answer, and has the answer to all our questions. Look no further than to Jesus. If we acknowledge Him in all our ways, He will direct our paths.

Mission

Look up.

Daily Notes: _____

_____

_____

_____

_____

_____

_____

_____

ACKNOWLEDGE

Acknowledge: to admit to be real to true; recognize the existence, truth, or fact of:

> **Proverbs 3:6** — *In all thy ways acknowledge him, and he shall direct thy paths.*

Testimony

Before I was saved there were things I thought I wanted. Once I got them, I realized they didn't make me happy, or they ended up not being as good as I thought they would be. Once I started serving the Lord and started acknowledging Him in all my ways, I ended up in places I never thought I would go. I became friends with people I couldn't imagine being friends with. And I married the love of my life. The Lord has big plans for us. Let's not miss them!

Mission

Acknowledge Him.

Daily Notes: _____

_____

_____

_____

_____

_____

_____

_____

_____

_____

ARISE

August 10

Arise: to get up from sitting, lying, or kneeling; rise

> **Ruth 1:20** — *And she said unto them, Call me not Naomi, call me Mara: for the Almighty hath dealt very bitterly with me.*

Testimony

Naomi didn't arise above the problems she was facing; instead she changed her name to Mara and renamed her situation. She spoke over her life that the Lord had *dealt bitterly against her*. Does the Lord ever deal bitterly against us? Does the Lord ever cause evil to fall upon us? Of course NOT! The Lord only has good plans for us. When the sin of this world and circumstances happen, we can turn to the Lord to help us overcome them. Naomi ended up overcoming her situation once she acknowledged the Lord. Don't let your situation overcome you. Instead, overcome your situation with Jesus.

Mission

Change the name of your situation to glorify the Lord.

Daily Notes: _____

_____

_____

_____

_____

_____

_____

ABODE

August 11

Abode: a place in which a person resides; home

> **Galatians 4:6** — *And because ye are sons, God hath sent forth the Spirit of his Son into your hearts, crying Abba, Father.*

Testimony

When you accepted Jesus and asked Him to come into your hearts and received salvation, you were given His Spirit at that moment. The Holy Spirit lives inside of your heart. What kind of place is the Holy Spirit abiding in? Are you providing a good home for the Holy Spirit? We need to make sure what we're doing is lining up with the Word. The Holy Spirit lives inside of us.

Mission

Provide a good home for the Holy Spirit to abide.

Daily Notes: _____

_____

_____

_____

_____

_____

_____

_____

_____

_____

_____

ADJOURN

August 12

Adjourn: to defer or postpone to a later time.

2 Timothy 4:7 — *I have fought a good fight, I have finished my course, I have kept the faith:*

Testimony

Don't adjourn the opportunities God gives you. Don't adjourn growing in the Lord. Now is the time because we're not promised our next breath. At the end of each day, be able to say *I have fought the good fight, finished, and kept the faith.*

Mission

Live each day like it's your last, because it could be.

Daily Notes: _____

_____

_____

_____

_____

_____

_____

_____

_____

_____

_____

_____

_____

_____

APPREHEND

August 13

Apprehend: to grasp the meaning of; understand

2 Timothy 3:16 — *All scripture is given by inspiration of God, and is profitable for doctrine, for reproof, for correction, for instruction in righteousness:*

Testimony

We have to apprehend and believe that all scripture was inspired by God, because it was. We have to strive not to twist scripture to fit our needs. Each scripture was inspired by the Lord and written to help us in every area of life leading us to eternal life. Don't doubt or ever question God's Word. Know that men wrote the scripture under the influence of the Holy Spirit and God approved every word written. Accept the Word and don't try to fit it into a gray area of your life. It's clear and simple, black or white, with what God is speaking to you concerning your situation.

Mission

Don't twist God's Word once you apprehend it. Accept it. Live by it. Move on and grow.

Daily Notes: _____

_____

_____

_____

_____

_____

_____

_____

ABNEGATION

August 14

Abnegation: denying oneself some rights, or conveniences

Hebrew 13:21 — *Make you perfect in every good work to do his will, working in you that which is well pleasing in his sight, through Jesus Christ; to whom be glory for ever and ever Amen.*

Testimony

Don't deny yourself the privilege of Jesus wanting to be part of every aspect of your life. Jesus wants to meet every need and meet you at every place in your life. He wants to bring you out of darkness and into His glory. Jesus will supply and meet every need in your life. You have to let him. Don't deny yourself the love Jesus wants to give you. Don't deny yourself the pleasures and the blessings Jesus is just waiting to pour out on you. You are worthy of it all.

Mission

Don't deny.

Daily Notes: _____

_____

_____

_____

_____

_____

_____

_____

_____

ALACRITY

August 15

Alacrity: cheerful readiness, promptness, or willingness:

> **2 Thessalonians 3:10** — *For even when we were with you, this we commanded you, that if any would not work, neither should he eat.*

Testimony

We have to use what the Lord gives us — our health, mind, resources, and children. We need to work and do our best to glorify Him with everything the Lord has given us. Idle hands are the devil's favorite tool.

Scripture tells us if we don't work, we will not eat. We have to work unto the Lord and not unto man, and use what the Lord has given us to best glorify Him. Do not become idle in your work — whether you're a stay-at-home dad or mom, waitress or waiter, teacher, doctor, or construction worker. Whatever work the Lord has lined up for you to do, do it to the best of your ability and do it to glorify Him with alacrity. God commands us to work. The consequences of taking what God has given us and becoming lazy, may result in your not eating. That's how important it is to use what the Lord has given you.

Mission

Work.

Daily Notes: _____

_____

_____

_____

_____

AUGMENT

August 16

Augment: to make larger; enlarge in size, number, strength, or extent; increase

Judges 7:4 — *And the Lord said unto Gideon, the people are yet too many; bring them down unto the water, and I will try them for thee there, and it shall be, that of whom I say unto thee, This shall go with thee the same shall go with thee; and of whomsoever I say unto thee, This shall not go with thee, the same shall not go.*

Testimony

Gideon selected an army to augment his existing army. God selected an army of a smaller size. Gideon's army was way too large. God's army was small. Jesus has a way of making big things happen in small spaces. Jesus doesn't need an army of augment to make something happen in your life. The army God selected wasn't of augment; but it was powerful because He chose it. Jesus chooses you too. You might not think you have what it takes, but Jesus does.

Mission

Let God work in every area of your life. He can make big things happen in small spaces.

Daily Notes: _____

_____

_____

_____

_____

_____

AGGLOMERATION

August 17

Agglomeration: a jumbled cluster or mass of varied parts.

Nehemiah 6:15 — *So the wall was finished in the twenty and fifth day of the month Elul, in fifty and two days.*

Testimony

God called Nehemiah to rebuild the walls of Jerusalem. Nehemiah was the cupbearer to the King so he had the Kings trust. However, Nehemiah had to face many tasks before building the wall. One task was getting the king's permission to build the wall. He faced harassment and reforms from the people. I am sure there were times when the wall laid in an agglomeration. Nehemiah could have looked at the parts of the wall laying everywhere and thought, "I'll never finish this." Instead, Nehemiah was able to accomplish the task of rebuilding the wall in record time. He was consistent. He didn't lose focus on the task God had given him. He stayed in prayer, praying for God to strengthen his hands. When God's in it, you won't fail. Pray for God to show you what He wants you to do. When He speaks, be like Nehemiah, go and accomplish the task God gives you. Let nothing stop you.

Mission

52 days was a record time for rebuilding the wall. Keep praying and keep going on with the task God has given you.

Daily Notes: _____

_____

_____

_____

_____

AUTHORITY

August 18

Authority: the power to determine, adjudicate, or otherwise settle issues or disputes.

> **Mark 16:16-18** — *He that believeth and is baptized shall be saved; but he that believeth not shall be damned. And these signs shall follow them that believe; In my name shall they cast out devils; they shall speak with new tongues; They shall take up serpents; and if they drink any deadly thing, it shall not hurt them; they shall lay hands on the sick, and they shall recover.*

Testimony

Jesus gives us authority over darkness in our lives. Jesus is the authority over everything. Don't you realize the power you have in the name of Jesus? You have the authority to put Jesus in the middle of our darkness, saying in faith, "Get out of here satan, in the name of Jesus," and he has to flee. Those that believe and have Christ living inside of them have authority through Jesus to cast out devils, lay hands on the sick, and pray for healing. We have to believe that. We have the power to do what scripture says. Jesus is our authority. He is the authority over every situation in our lives.

Mission

Claim Jesus as authority over every decision and every aspect of your life.

Daily Notes: _____

_____

_____

_____

APPOINTED

August 19

Appointed: predetermined; arranged; set:

Mark 1:41 — *And Jesus, moved with compassion, put forth his hand, and touched him, and saith unto him, I will; be thou clean.*

Testimony

You were appointed for such a time as this. You were appointed by God to do the things He has you doing in your life. It wasn't by consequence, or by accident, that you first heard of His love and asked Him to save you. That day was appointed by Jesus. When the leper was healed, do you think it was a consequence because "Jesus was just walking by?" Jesus knew where he was going and what he was doing. The leper had an appointed time with Jesus and he was healed.

Mission

Think about the appointed time when you first came to know Jesus. Share that testimony with others.

Daily Notes: _____

_____

_____

_____

_____

_____

_____

_____

_____

ASHDODITES

August 20

Ashdodites: inhabitants of ASHDOD

Nehemiah 4:7 — *But it came to pass that when Sanballat, and Tobiah, and the Arabians, and the Ammonities, and the Ashdodites, heard that the walls of Jerusalem were made up, and that the breaches began to be stopped, then they were very wroth.*

Testimony

The Ashdodities were a group who joined the alliance that threatened the wall that was being built. When we join a group of new friends, or move to a new neighborhood, we can either help or hinder that group. The Ashdodities were part of the group that was a threat. We should know that nothing can stop God's plan. God is bigger than any threat we could ever receive when doing His will. How will you encourage others when they are doing the work of the Lord? Your actions speak louder than words. Will you help or hinder the vision that God has given them? You can either be a part of the blessing or not. The choice is yours.

Mission

Help the group you're a part of. Don't hinder!

Daily Notes: _____

_____

_____

_____

_____

_____

ARAH

Arah: one of his descendants, Shechaniah, the son of Arah.

> **Nehemiah 6:16** — *And it came to pass, that when all our enemies heard thereof, and all the heathen that were about us saw these things, they were much cast down in their own eyes: for they perceived that this work was wrought of our God.*

Testimony

Nehemiah married the daughter of Shechaniah who was the son of Arah. This arrangement caused information to leak, which lead Tobiah to send letters to Nehemiah, making him fearful. Instead of giving reference to God for divinely completing the rebuilding of the wall in fifty-two days, they wanted to promote themselves. Because the rebuilding of the wall was an incredible task, they had to take their eyes off themselves and acknowledge God as having played a part in this. There was no denying the Lord's part in rebuilding this wall.

We all know people who acknowledge the Lord for helping in hard times. Once the trial is over, they forget and say, "I did this." They forget that the Lord was in control the whole time. Sometimes we give glory to God in the middle of a trial, but once it's over, we forget the magnificence of what God truly did. So adjust your eyes. Give God glory because He is in control of all. You may think you had something to do with it, but God created you and gave you the ability to work through the trial. We have to get to a point where we thank God continuously and realize that it's not about us at all. Instead, it's all about what God has given us and what He is doing through us.

Mission

Give credit where credit is due. God deserves it all.

Daily Notes: _____

_____

AIJA

August 22

Aija: A form of a name for a city Ai.

> **Nehemiah 11:31** — *The children also of Benjamin from Geba dwelt at Michmash, and Aija, and Bethel and in their villages.*

Testimony

In Nehemiah chapter eleven there is plan for resettlement among the people of Jerusalem — a plan for resettlement within Jerusalem and a plan for resettlement outside of Jerusalem. Aija was a village outside of Jerusalem. In your life, whether you're in a state of being "in" or "out" of a situation, you must know that Jesus has a plan to settle you, pick you up, and put you on solid ground. Jesus has blessings and a plan for your life. Regardless of being in or out of a marriage, in or out of a crowd, life's coming together or life's falling apart, Jesus has a plan to settle you.

Mission

Call upon Jesus to settle all things. Don't leave Him out.

Daily Notes: _____

_____

_____

_____

_____

_____

_____

_____

_____

AUTHOR

August 23

Author: a person who writes

Ecclesiastes 3:1 — *To everything there is a season, and a time to every purpose under the heaven:*

Testimony

I happen to know one author in my life and she's the reason you're reading this devotional book now. She is an author of many Christian study guides as well as a speaker, sister, and friend. God puts people in your life for His purpose and perfect timing. There is a purpose for everything. God knew that I would need this person in my life to help me accomplish the plans He has for me. God has put people in your life, too. It might not be an author; it might be a teacher, boss, spouse, stranger, or friend. These people have a purpose for being in your life. God has placed them in your life for a reason — a lesson learned or a lesson taught. Whatever the reason is, make sure it glorifies the Lord. Make sure all your relationships are based on Jesus so they will last and God will be glorified. That is most certainly what my relationship is like with this author, sister, and friend.

Mission

Let these people in your life know how special they are, and don't forget to thank Jesus for placing them in your life!

Daily Notes: _____

_____

_____

_____

_____

AUTHORSHIP

August 24

Authorship: reference to an author, creator, or producer

Romans 13:1 — *Let every soul be subject unto the higher powers: For there is no power but of God: the powers that be are ordained of God.*

Testimony

God is our author and we are His authorship. God is the only One who is in control. We need to realize that and give reference to our author — our creator of Heaven and of Earth. God spoke and it was. Jesus is all powerful and in control of every aspect of our lives. Don't fear. The thing you fear has no control over Jesus. Worry ends where faith begins. Recognize Jesus as the author and finisher of your faith.

Mission

Let Jesus be your author.

Daily Notes: _____

_____

_____

_____

_____

_____

_____

_____

_____

_____

_____

ABUSES

August 25

Abuses: to use wrongly or improperly; misuse

1 Corinthians 5:6 — *our glorying is not good. Know ye not that a little leaven leaveneth the whole lump?*

Testimony

I read a sign on a church one day, and when I saw it I prayed, "Jesus, please don't let me ever forget that!" The sign said, "Give the devil an inch and he will become your ruler." Separate yourself from your sin and the sins of others. Where sin is, the devil reigns. Separate yourself from your sins, your secret sins that only maybe you know about. Get rid of them. Separate yourselves from those living and actively participating in sin. You can't keep putting yourself in the position to sin. If you surround yourself with darkness, the whole of who you are will become contaminated. Keep yourself in the presence of Jesus and surround yourself with like-minded believers who will encourage and lift you up on your walk with the Lord. Pray to be in God's will daily.

Mission

Get out of the gray area of your life, before the whole lump is leavened.

Daily Notes: _____

_____

_____

_____

_____

_____

_____

ADJUDICATE

August 26

Adjudicate: to settle or determine an issue or dispute.

1 Corinthians 7:2 — Nevertheless, to avoid fornication, let every man have his own wife, and every woman have her own husband.

Testimony

Jesus gave specific instructions to adjudicate married life. If you are engaged or entering into a marriage, you need to know what Jesus teaches and expects out of a marriage. Beyond marriage we need to let Jesus adjudicate every issue in our lives. If we want to live and act in a way that lines up with the Word of God, we have to put Jesus in every situation. If you find yourself wondering, "Am I doing the right things or am I in the right situation?" Look at what Jesus has to say about what you should be doing in your life. You will find that Jesus gives specific instructions concerning every issue we will ever face. It's all found in His Word. Take God's Word very seriously. Go to God's Word first. Let God's Word adjudicate every issue you will ever face.

Mission

Let Jesus adjudicate your issues in life.

Daily Notes: _____

_____

_____

_____

_____

_____

_____

ATTENTIVE

August 27

Attentive: characterized by or giving attention; observant:

Philippians 4:19 — *But my God shall supply all your need according to his riches in glory by Christ Jesus.*

Testimony

Isn't it great to know that Jesus is attentive to every need we have and ever will have in the future? Not only is He attentive, but He will also supply! If that doesn't get you excited today, then you might be lost! You are serving a living Savior who will supply all your needs. He knows what you need before you do.

Mission

Get excited knowing that your needs are met!

Daily Notes: _____

_____

_____

_____

_____

_____

_____

_____

_____

_____

_____

_____

_____

ACCORDING

August 28

According: agreeing

> **Philippians 4:13** — *I can do all things through Christ which strengtheneth me.*

Testimony

According to Jesus, we can do all things! According to your living Savior, nothing can stop you. God wants our trust, not our questions. Know that the God you serve can make all things happen through you. You can do all things. Get excited at the fact that according to Jesus, you are His; a child of God who can do all things.

Mission

Believe in Jesus and know that, according to Jesus, you can do all things.

Daily Notes: _____

_____

_____

_____

_____

_____

_____

_____

_____

_____

APPERTAINED

August 29

Appertained: to belong as a part, right, possession, or attribute.

Nehemiah 2:8 — *And a letter unto Asaph the keeper of the kings forest, that he may give me timber to make beams for the gates of the palace which appertained to the house, and for the wall of the city, and for the house that I shall enter into. And the king granted me, according to the good hand of my God upon me.*

Testimony

Nehemiah got all that appertained to the wall being built. When he got it all, he acknowledged the Lord. He saw that the Lord's good hand was upon him. Everything fell into place and the king granted Nehemiah permission to start rebuilding the wall. When we follow God's plan — however big, crazy, or small it might be — we will appertain all that we need to see the task completed. We have to remember Nehemiah, and every step of the way give credit to God. If Nehemiah credited himself for the wall or tried to seek glory for himself, he would not have gone very far. God's Word tells us that without Him, we can do nothing. We need to remember that God's plans are better than ours; and God will make sure that we have appertained all that we need to accomplish His will for our lives.

Mission

Give God glory — not just at the beginning or end — but give God glory every step of the way, like Nehemiah did.

Daily Notes: _____

_____

_____

ARTAXERXES

August 30

Artaxerxes: a king of Persia

Nehemiah 2:2 — *Wherefore the king said unto me, Why is thy countenance sad, seeing thou art not sick? This is nothing else but sorrow of heart. Then I was very sore afraid.*

Testimony

Nehemiah had to get the king's permission to rebuild the wall. Nehemiah was nervous, much like any of us are when we have to get permission for anything we want to do. Nehemiah had God on his side. The Lord had prepared Artaxerxes' heart to assign Nehemiah the task of rebuilding the wall. He also granted supplies to help him with this task.

When God is for us, who can be against us? When Jesus has a plan and we fall into submission to it, He prepares the hearts of people we encounter along the way. Nothing will stop God's plans for your life. Artaxerxes' heart was prepared for Nehemiah to fulfill his calling.

Mission

Ask Jesus to prepare the hearts of those you come into contact with.

Daily Notes: _____

_____

_____

_____

_____

_____

AUGUST

August 31

Reflection of the month of August:

Nehemiah 2:20 — *Then answered I them, and said unto them, The God of Heaven, he will prosper us; therefore we his servants will arise and build: but ye have no portion, nor right, nor memorial, in Jerusalem.*

Testimony

This is how Nehemiah answers his enemies. He doesn't defend himself or become prideful when his enemies are attacking him and laughing at his plan. He acknowledges that he is just a servant of the Lord, doing what God has called him to do. He acknowledges who will prosper him. We need to remember Nehemiah's example and how he answered his enemies. We need to be ready to give an answer to our enemies. When that time comes, be like Nehemiah and acknowledge the Lord for all He has done. Nehemiah said what he was going to do and who was helping him do it. Don't make it about yourself. Make it all about Jesus, and watch your enemies flee.

Mission

How did you answer people that caused frustrations in your life this month? If you became prideful or defensive, remember who is fighting your battles. When you give your battle to Jesus, you don't have to fight. He will fight for you. Make sure that you strive to acknowledge the Lord and point your enemies towards Jesus.

Daily Notes: _____

_____

_____

SOURCES

September 1

Sources: a source of supply, support, or aid, especially one that can be readily drawn upon when needed.

> **John 4:47** — *When he heard that JESUS was come out of Judea into Galilee, he went unto Him, and besought Him that He would come down, and heal his son: for he was at the point of death.*

Testimony

If the nobleman had not used the resources available to him, his son would have died. JESUS is our main resource. Let Him be your 'go-to' source in every area of your life. JESUS will aid and supply in every problem you will ever face. He is the best source. He is always available and waiting to be called upon.

Mission

When you find yourself in need, make JESUS your first resource — not your last resort.

Daily Notes: _____

_____

_____

_____

_____

_____

_____

_____

_____

SELFLESS

September 2

Selfless: having little or no concern for oneself, especially with regard to fame, position, or money.

1 Peter 5:6 — *Humble yourselves therefore under the mighty hand of God, that he may exalt you in due time.*

Testimony

My sister-in-law, Codi Gandee, wrote the book *Selfless in a Selfie World.* The book is all about being humble and how Jesus humbled Himself, to the point of death on the cross, for us. Jesus was selfless, and we are to follow his example of selflessness and humility. My sister-in-law does a great job of demonstrating exactly what her book teaches. If it weren't for her selflessness, the devotional you're reading today wouldn't have been possible. Take a look at yourself. How selfless are you? In what areas of your life could you be more humble? Our goal as Christians should be to be selfless enough so that when people look at us, they see Jesus.

Mission

Jesus was humble. We should be also.

Daily Notes: _____

_____

_____

_____

_____

_____

_____

STUDY

September 3

Study: application of the mind to the acquisition of knowledge, as by reading, investigation, or reflection.

Colossians 4:6 — *Let your speech be always with grace, seasoned with salt, that ye may know how ye ought to answer every man.*

Testimony

We want our mouths and our words to be full of the Word. How do we get to the point of knowing that our speech is full of grace and seasoned so we can answer every man? We study the Word. We have to make time to study and spend time with our Savior. The Word teaches us grace, how we should speak, how we should treat others, and what we should do. The bottom line is: we would be lost without it. All advice for dealing with any situation you encounter is available in the Word. Jesus gives us step-by-step instructions for living in His Word, but if we don't study it, how will we ever know it? How will we know if what we are doing is lining up with the Word of God? The only way to know is to study His Word while asking Jesus to instruct you and guide you in your study time.

Mission

Study the Word.

Daily Notes: _____

_____

_____

_____

_____

SCRIPTURE

September 4

Scripture: the sacred writings of the Old and New Testaments.

2 Timothy 3:16 — *All scripture is given by inspiration of God, and is profitable for doctrine, for reproof, for correction, for instruction in righteousness.*

Testimony

All scripture was given by inspiration of God; not just certain parts of it — the parts you want to choose to live by and the other parts you choose to ignore. It doesn't work that way. We can't pick and choose. The Lord gave it all to us. It is all profitable and righteous, and can be used to help us. Sometimes we compromise on some of the scripture and choose to focus only on the certain parts that we can easily fulfill. God gave it all to us. Some parts of the Bible may seem impossible to follow, and it is. That's the point. In John 15:5 it says that *without Jesus we can do nothing*. We need Jesus. With Jesus it is possible to love your enemies, and do good to them that hate you. We cannot compromise any longer. When we stand up for the Word of God, we are saying to the devil, "I'm not compromising; not today!" That's not being opinionated or judgmental. We are simply standing up for the Word of God like Jesus wants us to. Obey all the scriptures. You do that with Jesus because by yourself, you will not be able to. Jesus makes all things possible and new. You can live up to each and every word in scripture through Jesus.

Mission

Read it all.

Daily Notes: _____

_____

STRENGTH

September 5

Strength: the quality or state of being strong; mental power, force, or vigor.

> **Judges 16:6** — *And Delilah said to Samson, Tell me, I pray thee, wherein thy great strength lieth, and wherewith thou mightiest be bound to afflict thee.*

Testimony

Samson was a man of great physical strength, but his mental strength failed him. His mental strength was so weak that it cost him his wife, his eyes, everything. Disobedience to God's plan eventually led to his death. We have to have strong mental strength. A weak mind is a playground for satan. Satan will use what he can to get you to disobey God. In Samson's case, satan used his strength against him. The thing that God blessed Samson with is what satan used against him. Sound familiar? Satan wants to destroy God's plan for your life and all the blessings the Lord has given you. Surrender everything to Jesus, and pray for your mind to be strengthened with the things of God instead of things of this world. Samson let his mind and his flesh think on things of the world. The consequence for not having a mind that was strengthened by the Lord was death.

Mission

Pray for the Lord to strengthen your mind so you will be equipped to do His will. Resist the temptations of the world.

Daily Notes: _____

_____

_____

_____

SELFIE

September 6

Selfie: a photograph taken with a smartphone or other digital camera by a person who is also in the photograph.

> **Colossians 3:23-24** — *And whatsoever ye do, do it heartily, as to the Lord, and not unto men; knowing that of the Lord ye shall receive the reward of the inheritance: for ye serve the Lord Christ.*

Testimony

A lot of selfies consist of people making various faces, at different places, with different people. A selfie tells us exactly what you are doing and a lot about who you are. If you had to think of an overall 'life' selfie, what would it look like? Who would be in it? In the midst of a selfish, selfie world, it's easy to get caught up in the world instead of focusing on the Lord. If the Lord was to take a selfie of me or you, what would it look like? What would it say? The Lord has so much love for me and you; a selfie from Him couldn't contain all the beautiful things He has given us. Its humbling to think of how much the Lord loves us, and all the good thoughts He thinks towards us. When I think of a selfie with the Lord, I see the words *overcomer, beautiful, powerful, loved, blessed, forgiven,* and *redeemed* spread out all over the selfie photo.

The next time you take a selfie, let it be a reminder of who you serve and who has created you. The next time you take a selfie with another person, thank the Lord for that person — your brother or sister in Christ if they are serving Jesus. Lastly, the next time you take a selfie in some place, take the time to look around and thank God for His beautiful creation and people He has made. Be selfless in your selfie and think of the Lord. Show others how good He is to you. Jesus created you. Include Jesus in your selfie world.

Mission

Be selfless in your selfie.

Daily Notes: _____

_____

_____

_____

_____

_____

_____

_____

_____

_____

_____

_____

_____

_____

_____

_____

_____

_____

_____

_____

_____

_____

_____

_____

STEAL

September 7

Steal: to take the property of another or others.

> **Proverbs 3:9** — *Honor the Lord with thy substance, and with the first fruits of all thine increase.*

> **Leviticus 27:30** — *And all the tithe of the land, whether of the seed of the land, or of the fruit of the tree, is the Lords, it is holy unto the Lord.*

Testimony

Everything we have belongs to the Lord, on loan to us. God gives us 100 percent, so why is it hard for us to tithe 10 percent to Him and give additional for offerings? We need to remember that keeping what God requires is actually stealing from God. He owns it all, and he freely gives it to us. Why not, then, give back to the Lord what is already His?

I had never really tithed correctly until I got married and my husband started tithing! At first, we felt like it was just another bill, but then it became more. We started giving with a cheerful heart, and the Lord blessed us beyond anything we could ever given Him. My husband got promotions and I got jobs left and right. God truly took care of us beyond anything we could have asked for. Give to the Lord; He will bless you for it. Giving is an opportunity for you to glorify God with the finances He has given you.

Mission

Don't steal from God. Instead give back what He gave you.

Daily Notes: _____

_____

_____

STAND

September 8

Stand: to be in an upright position on the feet.

Psalm 18:2 — *The Lord is my rock, and my fortress, and my deliver; my God, my strength, in whom I will trust; my buckler, and the horn of my salvation, and my high tower.*

Testimony

There is a woman in my church that has such a powerful testimony that all she has to do is stand. She is a true, walking testimony of God's love and what He has brought her through. When she stands, you know that she is standing on rock, solid ground. Jesus Christ is whom she stands upon; whom she trusts; and whom she gets her strength from. Standing on God's Word and knowing who is holding you is enough to make the devil flee. He has to go if Jesus is the rock and the ground you're standing. Know where you stand with Jesus. You are a child of God. If you can't speak, just make sure you stand on Jesus. He will lift you up.

Mission

Just stand.

Daily Notes: _____

_____

_____

_____

_____

_____

_____

STABILITY

September 9

Stability: state or quality of being stable.

> **Psalm 18:32** — *It is God that girdeth me with strength, and maketh my way perfect.*

Testimony

Aren't you glad that Jesus is constant? Jesus is our stability! I'm glad that I am not in this world alone. I'm glad to have a Savior who is personal, as close as a best friend, a dear father who is strengthening me and who makes my paths straight and perfect. If you feel like you're unstable, get out of this world and focus on the Word. We have a lot of ups and downs in life, but we can count on Jesus to bring us out of whatever we're going through and put us on solid, stable ground.

Mission

Pray for Jesus to bring you to a state of stability.

Daily Notes: _____

_____

_____

_____

_____

_____

_____

_____

_____

_____

STUMBLING

September 10

Stumbling: to walk or go unsteadily.

Romans 14:13 — *Let us not therefore judge one another anymore: but judge this rather, that no man put a stumbling block or an occasion to fall in his brothers way.*

Testimony

What's that thing in your life that keeps you from going all in and serving the Lord fully? What is the stumbling block in your life that keeps you from absolutely doing everything Jesus wants you to do every part of the day? Whatever it is, get rid of it. If you want to see Jesus move in a big way in your life, then get rid of the stumbling blocks. Let Jesus turn them into stepping stones for His glory. Don't stand in the way of others, either. Instead of being a stumbling block, be an encourager to whoever is trying to do the things that Jesus wants them to do. It doesn't matter if you like it or not. If it brings God glory, get out of the way. Paul rejoiced in the truth, not in what was going on. It's all about Jesus. Get rid of the stumbling blocks in your life so you can just run to Him, and do all the things He has called you to do. Lift yourself and others up.

Mission

Step over the stumbling blocks.

Daily Notes: _____

_____

_____

_____

_____

SPECIAL

September 11

Special: being a particular one

John 15:16 — *Ye have not chosen me, but I have chosen you, and ordained you, that ye should go and bring forth fruit, and that your fruit should remain; that whatsoever ye shall ask of the Father in my name, he may give it you.*

Testimony

You are special. Jesus chose you. For the longest time I thought there was a point in my life when I chose Him. Once I started studying the word and spending time with my Savior, I realized He chose all of us. We are special to Him. He picked us. Have you ever been the kid on the bench at school that was picked last? Jesus always picks us first; we are never last with Jesus. We are of top importance, first and foremost, to Him. We are His beloved children. He wants to be special in our lives, too. We have to prioritize and put Jesus first. We are special to Him, but He is most certainly special to us. What a special, personal relationship!

Mission

Show and tell the entire world that Jesus chose us. We are special because we are His children.

Daily Notes: _____

_____

_____

_____

_____

_____

_____

SHINE

September 12

Shine: to give forth with light to glow or cast.

Matthew 5:16 — *Let your light so shine before men, that they may see your good works, and glorify your Father which is in heaven.*

Testimony

My husband lets his light shine. When we first got together, I wasn't serving the Lord. When we broke up, there were many times I backslid and didn't serve the Lord then, either. Being around my husband, just watching the way his light shines, the way he serves the Lord with seriousness, and the way he treats others, makes me want to be better. Being around him makes me want to serve the Lord even fuller. His light is bright. I encourage you to find someone—a friend, spouse, or relative—that you can be around that has a bright light. Find that person because it will bring light into the dark areas of your own life.

My husband's uncle has led church services many times at our church. Once, he lit one little match in a dark room and it lit up the entire room. He went on to explain that that's how it is when we are serving the Lord. A little bit of light can shine light on a whole lot of darkness. So, let it shine people! Let it shine!

Mission

Let your light shine bright for the entire world to see.

Daily Notes: _____

_____

_____

_____

_____

SHARE

September 13

Share: a full or proper portion.

> **James 2:19** — *Thou believest that there is one God; thou doest well: the devils also believe, and tremble.*

Testimony

It is not enough just to believe and acknowledge. The demons in hell actually tremble because they believe, but they lack saving faith and trust in Jesus — the salvation of Jesus Christ. Share and spread the gospel of Christ. Share everything you know with everybody you know about Jesus. It takes faith and acceptance of Christ. We don't want people to be unbelieving, like the demons. We have to share Jesus and let everyone know that Jesus is enough; He is everything. We need to accept Him, believe in His sacrifice, and ask him to come abide in our hearts. Jesus is everything. He is enough. Share that good news.

Mission

Share your testimony. Make the devils in hell tremble.

Daily Notes: _____

_____

_____

_____

_____

_____

_____

_____

_____

SAVINGS

September 14

Savings: tending to serve to save; rescuing; preserving.

Acts 28:3 — *And when Paul had gathered a bundle of sticks, and laid them on the fire, there came a viper out of the heat, and it fastened on his hand.*

Testimony

Paul should have died or had a reaction other than just shaking the viper into the fire. The barbarians on the island knew the snake was venomous and when Paul was unhurt and shook it off like nothing had happened, they knew there was something different about Paul. Their minds started to wonder and change. God had a plan for Paul being shipwrecked on that island. All the events that led up to Paul being on the island wasn't coincidental; it was the Lord getting Paul to where He wanted him to be. There was physical healing taking place on Paul after being shipwrecked and bitten by the snake. At the same time, there was a spiritual healing taking place in the minds and hearts of the barbarians on the island. God's plan for saving you and giving you life is no coincidence. Jesus will use whatever you've gone through to strengthen you to do His work. Be like Paul and shake off the snake. Get back to God's work that He planned for your life.

Mission

Shake the snakes off, and get busy about God's business. Jesus saving you wasn't a coincidence.

Daily Notes: _____

_____

_____

_____

SOULS

Souls: the spiritual part of humans as distinct from the physical part.

> **1 Samuel 18:1** — *And it came to pass, when he had made an end of speaking unto Saul, that the soul of Jonathan was knit with the soul of David, and Jonathan loved him as his own soul.*

Testimony

The type of friendship between Jonathan and David was only possible by the Lord blessing it. Jonathan was Saul's son and rightful heir to the throne. But God's plan was to make David the king. We can see from a worldly perspective how this could easily get ugly with comments like, "It's my right. It's mine." But instead of looking at himself, Jonathan looked to the Lord and was a humble man. He put his feelings aside and served the Lord fully. David and Jonathan had a bond, as they both were obedient to God's plan. God knit the souls of David and Jonathan so they would do His will. We see when we read the rest of the story that Jonathan gives over complete control to David. God prepared their hearts and souls to do His work. If your soul is bearing witness with another's, don't ignore it. Find out why the Lord has drawn that person or situation to you. Give God complete control and let Him prepare your heart, knitting it together with whomever God chooses to do His will.

Mission

Make sure your soul is knit with Jesus, and with whomever else Jesus wants in your life.

Daily Notes: _____

_____

SAND

Sand: the more or less fine debris or rocks, consisting of small, loose grains, often of quartz.

> **Psalm 139:17-18** — *How precious also are thy thoughts unto me, O God! How great is the sum of them! If I should count them, they are more in number than the sand: when I awake, I am still with thee.*

Testimony

When we see the sandy shore at the beach or sand along a lake or creek bank, it's almost impossible to count the grains of sand in front of us. The precious thoughts our Savior thinks towards us are more than the sand at the shore. We can't fully grasp how much Jesus loves us or how much He thinks about us. If you would sit down or look at the sand, it is unending and immeasurable like the thoughts Jesus has towards us. The loving, kind, peaceful, thoughts our loving Savior has towards us is full of so much love. The best part about it is, *it is real*. Our Savior is with us every single moment thinking good thoughts towards us every second of the day. If you're not feeling loved, think again and know Jesus loves you.

Mission

You are loved. Believe it. You are loved more than the sand on the seashore.

Daily Notes: _____

_____

_____

_____

SMASHED

September 17

Smashed: drunk

1 Samuel 1:13 — *Now Hannah, she spake in her heart; only her lips moved, but her voice was not heard: therefore Eli thought she had been drunken.*

Testimony

Can you imagine praising and pouring your heart out to the Lord to the point where people assumed you were drunk — completely *smashed* in today's terms? Scripture says that Hannah spoke in her heart, her lips moved, but her voice was not heard. Could you imagine what Hannah looked like if she were in front of you? The way Hannah looked was enough to make Eli think she was drunk. Hannah was truly pouring her heart out. Hannah wasn't doing lip service, or portraying someone else, or acting a certain way for attention. She was truly serving the Lord regardless of who was around. We can learn that from Hannah. It didn't matter if Eli thought she was drunk. When he asked her, she replied, "I have drunk neither wine nor strong drink, but have poured my soul before the Lord." Pour your souls out right now. Pour your souls out every chance you get to worship the Lord. Do it like no one else matters except for Jesus.

Mission

Who cares who is watching! Pour your heart out to the Lord.

Daily Notes: _____

_____

_____

_____

_____

SOUND

September 18

Sound: hearing

> **Daniel 5:5** — *In the same hour came forth fingers of a man's hand, and wrote over against the candlestick upon the plaister of the wall of the kings palace: and the king saw the part of the hand that wrote.*

Testimony

Can you imagine King Nebuchadnezzar hearing the sound of the handwriting on the wall? Reading this part of the Bible almost gives you an Edgar Allan Poe type feel that you experience from reading his poems; the creepiness of it all. The thought that comes to my mind is, "What does it take for the Lord to get my attention?" In the next, verse King Nebuchadnezzar's countenance was changed. His thoughts troubled him and he shook all over. Does the Lord have to go to these extremes to get our attention? It's sad to say, but in some areas of my life, probably so. We can learn from the many events in the king's life. The Lord will get our attention one way or another. Let us listen the first time so we won't have to be reminded again and again.

Mission

Listen to the sounds around you.

Daily Notes: _____

_____

_____

_____

_____

_____

SPARED

September 19

Spared: to refrain from harming or destroying

> **2 Peter 2:5** — *And spared not the old world, but saved Noah the eighth person, a preacher of righteousness, bringing in the flood upon the world of the ungodly;*

Testimony

God spared Noah's life. Noah walked with the Lord and was a just man. The result of the flood brought death to all the wicked people on earth who sinned against God. God spared Noah, just like he will spare those of us who accept Him. Jesus spared us from the awful result of sin. Jesus did nothing wrong, but spared us from the cross and made a way for us to accept Him and have eternal life. What God did for Noah, he is doing for us today and for all who believe.

Mission

Thank Jesus for sparing your life by giving His.

Daily Notes: _____

_____

_____

_____

_____

_____

_____

_____

_____

SUSTAIN

September 20

Sustain: to support, hold, or bear up from below; bear the weight of

> **Matthew 27:51** — *And behold the veil of the temple was rent in twain from the top to the bottom; and the earth did quake, and the rocks rent;*

Testimony

Nothing could sustain the veil any longer. Jesus tore the veil in to, now giving us direct access to our Father, forever! The torn veil means we have direct access to our Lord and Savior whenever we want. We don't have to communicate through a prophet or the holiest of holies any longer! We ourselves can have a personal relationship with Jesus Christ. Speak to Him like He is your best friend, father, and Savior, because He is. Jesus tore the veil. Nothing in this world could ever sustain it. It's been torn once and for all.

Mission

Speak to Jesus. Nothing's stopping you!

Daily Notes: _____

_____

_____

_____

_____

_____

_____

_____

SILENT

September 21

Silent: making no sound

> **Proverbs 17:28** — *Even a fool, when he holdeth his peace, is counted wise: and he that shutteth his lips is esteemed a man of understanding.*

Testimony

Does the words you're speaking bring internal wounds? Our words carry much weight and speak volumes about who we are. We need to check our words before we speak. Are we speaking love, God's Word, and life; or are we speaking death and darkness? We need to think before we speak. According to God's Word, those who shut their lips are considered men of understanding. The words we speak need to line up with the Word of God. We need to consult God with the words we speak and make sure we are speaking the words He wants us to speak. Before opening our mouths into conversations or discussions, we need to pray for God's will to be done before we speak, using only the words approved by Him.

Mission

Allow God to control your mouth. If it's not from the Lord, stay silent.

Daily Notes: _____

_____

_____

_____

_____

_____

SEEKING

September 22

Seeking: to go in search or quest of

> **Matthew 7:7-8** — *Ask and it shall be given you; seek, and ye shall find; knock, and it shall be opened unto you: For everyone that asketh receiveth; and he that seeketh findeth; and to him that knocketh it shall be opened.*

Testimony

Whatever you're seeking, you're going to find it. If you're seeking to be judgmental or opinionated, that's what you're going to get. On the other hand, if you're seeking truth and Jesus, that's what you will find as well. What are you seeking? In your daily life what are you seeking out? Whatever you're seeking, you will find. Make sure you're seeking Jesus and His will for your life. You do not want anything less than God's best.

Mission

Seek God's best.

Daily Notes: _____

_____

_____

_____

_____

_____

_____

_____

_____

_____

SOFT

September 23

Soft: not hard or stiff

Proverbs 15:1 — *A soft answer turneth away wrath: but grievous words stir up anger.*

Testimony

Are you adding fuel to the flame in your life or are you extinguishing it? A lot of the times when we think back to confrontations, we can see how the argument possibly escalated from the words we spoke. In the midst of an argument, we need to speak with a soft answer. Pride gets in our way a lot of times and that just adds fuel to the flame as we become self-promoting. To line up with the Word of God, we can still speak the truth, but it must be done in love and with a soft answer. This helps keep the person you're speaking with from becoming angered and out of control. Ultimately, this helps you, too. By getting rid of your pride and providing a soft, loving answer in the midst of conflict, you're following God's Word and showing others Jesus. What's more important than that? You might be thinking, "You don't know my situation!" Your right! I don't, but Jesus does. He is the only one who can help us be more like Him, and less like our flesh wants us to be.

Mission

Ask Jesus to help you in the midst of angered feelings to provide soft answers that extinguish the fires in your life.

Daily Notes: _____

_____

_____

_____

SMOOTH

September 24

Smooth: free from projections or unevenness of surface; not rough: generally flat or unruffled, as a calm sea.

> **Psalm 107:29** — *He maketh the storm a calm, so that the waves thereof are still.*

Testimony

Jesus has been known to sleep during storms. If Jesus can sleep during storms, don't you think He can handle the storms in your life? Let Jesus smooth out the storms raging around you — internally and externally. Jesus not only makes the storm calm, but He controls the storm, is in the storm, and is already on the other side.

Mission

Call upon Jesus. He will smooth out the storm.

Daily Notes: _____

_____

_____

_____

_____

_____

_____

_____

_____

_____

_____

_____

STONE

September 25

Stone: the hard substance, formed of mineral matter, of which rocks consist.

John 8:7 — *So when they continued asking him, he lifted up himself, and said unto them, He that is without sin among you, let him first cast a stone at her.*

Testimony

In this well-known story, Jesus is put to the test. Jesus obviously passes every test He is ever put in. In this case, the scribes and Pharisees brought unto Him an adulterous woman. In order to catch her in adultery, they had to watch her every move to actually catch her in the act. What were they doing, looking in the windows? Following her every day waiting for her to mess up? Did they set up the scenario just to catch her? We don't know. What we can learn from them is instead of trying to catch people in the act or point out their faults, we need to be forgiving. Like Jesus said, "Who among you is without sin? Let him throw the first stone." None were left. Jesus then told the woman, "Go and sin no more." It is important for us to remember that verse, because like the adulterous woman, we have been forgiven of our sins. Let's not use Jesus as a monopoly "get out of jail free card." Let's not abuse Jesus' forgiveness and love. When Jesus forgives us of our sins, He also calls us out of that old life to live a new one with Him.

Mission

Go and sin no more.

Daily Notes: _____

_____

_____

SAFETY

Safety: the state of being safe.

> **Jeremiah 29:11** — *For I know the thoughts that I think toward you, saith the LORD, thoughts of peace, and not of evil, to give you an expected end.*

Testimony

When my niece started school, she got the job of being the light switch helper. Her mother always taught her to turn the lights off when leaving the room. Since she had instruction on this over and over, her mother made the comment to her, "See, I have been preparing you for this job your entire life." As funny as this situation is, we can apply it to our own lives with the Lord. The Lord knows the thoughts He has towards us; thoughts of peace and preparation for an expected end. Aren't you glad the events that take place in our lives are preparing us for future events or jobs the Lord has for us? Aren't you glad that you're safe in the Lord's embrace? Whatever is going on in your life right now, the Lord knows about it. Better yet, not only does He know, He also thinks thoughts of peace towards you.

Whatever is going on in your life right now, Jesus can use it in your future. You are safe in His arms.

Mission

Make Jesus your safe haven every day.

Daily Notes: _____

_____

_____

_____

_____

SISTER

Sister: a female sibling

> **1 Corinthians 1:10** — *Now I beseech you, brethren, by the name of our Lord Jesus Christ, that ye all speak the same thing, and that there be no divisions among you; but that ye be perfectly joined together in the same mind and in the same judgment.*

Testimony

I, myself, don't have any biological sisters, but I do have many sisters in Christ and two amazing sister-in-laws. In fact, it doesn't really feel right to put the "in laws" behind "sister," so let's just say they are my sisters. Many of you know how I feel or what I mean by that statement. So whether you have a sister, or a sister in Christ, you can relate to this daily word — sister. When I started writing this daily word, my first thoughts were of my sister-in-laws. The statement that Paul makes about having *no divisions among you, but perfectly join together* reminds me of how my sister-in-laws and my husband's family accept me as one of their own. It also made me think of my sisters in Christ — some that I've met at conferences or while visiting churches, and others that are by my side praying with me. God gave me good Christian friends and sisters in Christ. Jesus placed these "sisters" in your life. Do not let satan or the world throw any divisions among you. Instead, pray for them, protect them, and don't take advantage of them. Value your sisters and your sisters in Christ.

Mission

Praise God and thank Him for the "sisters" in your life.

Daily Notes: _____

_____

SHELTER

September 28

Shelter: something beneath, behind, or with in which a person, animal, or thing is protected from storms, missiles, adverse conditions, or a refuge.

> **Jonah 2:1** — *Then Jonah prayed unto the Lord his God out of the fish's belly.*

Testimony

We would typically never think of shelter being a fish's belly. For Jonah, the fish's belly was his shelter from the storm. I'm sure Jonah hated this shelter from the Lord. If our shelter — whether we like it or not — gets us into the will of God, it's worth it. How uncomfortable would Jonah have to be in his shelter before he would do what God would have him to do? We know Jonah hated the shelter that the Lord provided because he prayed, "Out of the belly of hell I cried, and thou heard my voice." Look around you. What is your shelter? Is the Lord trying to speak to you through the type of shelter He is providing in your life? If you're feeling like Jonah, cry out to the Lord. The Lord heard Jonah and the fish vomited him up onto dry land. Then Jonah went where the Lord wanted him to go. Cry out unto the Lord, but once the Lord provides — and he will — don't sit still and debate it. That kind of thinking is what got Jonah in the fish's belly to begin with. When Jesus answers, go where He wants you to go. He will change your shelter.

Mission

Walk towards the change.

Daily Notes: _____

_____

SMOKE

September 29

Smoke: the visible vapor and gases given off by a burning or smoldering substance.

> **Daniel 3:27** — *And the princes, governors, and captains, and the kings counselors, being gathered together, saw these men, upon whose bodies the fire had no power, nor was an hair of their head singed, neither were their coats changed, nor the smell of fire had passed on them.*

Testimony

They had just been in a fiery furnace! Where was the smoke? Where was the fire? When King Nebuchadnezzar threw them into the furnace, he looked into the fire and saw four men instead of three. He questioned those around him, "Didn't we throw three into the fire?" Jesus protected the three men. When they came out of the fire, they walked out in full flame; not physically, but spiritually. These men didn't even smell of smoke! They showed no physical side effects from being in a fire! That's how faithful and good Jesus is!

Mission

Come through the fire with Jesus. You won't even smell of smoke.

Daily Notes: _____

_____

_____

_____

_____

_____

SEPTEMBER

September 30

Reflection of the month of September:

Matthew 21:12-13 — *And Jesus went into the temple of God, and cast out all them that sold and bought in the temple, and overthrew the tables of the money changers, and the seats of them that sold doves, and said unto them, It is written, My house shall be called the house of prayer, but ye have made it a den of thieves.*

Testimony

Jesus was angry, but He did not sin. Jesus also didn't tolerate what was going on. We see that this behavior from Jesus demonstrated that He was angry and sinned not. The very next verse after this, Jesus heals the blind and lame in the temple. So not only did Jesus get rid of the bad behavior, he immediately showed them good. We can learn from this example. If something needs to be corrected, it's not enough just to say it's wrong. It's vital to show how to do it right. Jesus is the only perfect one. So we must consult Him on every decision before we make it. It's okay to be angry, but we have to learn from Jesus' example and sin not, showing the correct way to go and what to do. Jesus cleansed the temple. He didn't just point out the wrong and leave. He cleaned it up and showed what the temple needed to be used for. It was a house of prayer.

Cleanse the areas of your life. Jesus was perfect so He was able to do this for others. Before you go looking at others, look at yourself first. Cleanse yourself. Make sure every area of your life and heart is lining up with the Word of God. Ask Jesus to cleanse your heart like he cleansed the temple and be ready for correction and instruction from the Lord. Not only will He correct you, but He also won't leave you there. He'll show you and teach you the way to live, and what to do next.

Mission

Cleanse yourself. Think back, reflecting on this month. Do an overall evaluation on yourself. You know what needs to be cleansed in your life. Do it!

Daily Notes: _____

_____

_____

_____

_____

_____

_____

_____

_____

_____

_____

_____

_____

_____

_____

_____

_____

_____

_____

_____

_____

_____

_____

_____

OVERCOMER

Overcomer: to get the better of in a struggle or conflict; conquer; defeat.

> **Mark 6:56** — *And whithersoever he entered into villages, or cities, or country they laid the sick in the streets, and besought him that they might touch if it were but the boarder of his garment: and as many as touched him were made a whole.*

Testimony

All those who touched Jesus were made whole. What do the deaf, sick, blind, lost, diseased, broken, insane, and possessed have in common? We wouldn't typically look at these categories and think "overcomers," but with a touch from Jesus, they are more than overcomers. They were conquerors through Jesus Christ — completely healed and set free ready to testify of His greatness and glory. Jesus Christ is what they have in common. They once were broken, bound, and lost, but then Jesus touched them. They reached out and felt Jesus. Do you fall in the same category? They laid the sick in the streets so Jesus could heal them. How much faith did they have? You can reach out to Jesus today. If you only let him, He will make you an overcomer.

Mission

Be an overcomer through Jesus Christ.

Daily Notes: _____

_____

_____

_____

_____

OBEDIENCE

October 2

Obedience: the state or quality of being obedient.

> **Micah 7:18** — *Who is a God like unto thee, that pardoned iniquity, and passeth by the transgression of the remnant of his heritage? He retaineth not his anger forever, because he delighteth in mercy.*

Testimony

We should be obedient to what God wants us to do. But what happens when we're not obedient? Do we give up? Of course not! We fight the good fight and we don't give up. Obedience needs to be taught to us. Consequences follow at times when we aren't obedient to what God wants us to do. No matter what, don't give up. Keep going. We need to praise the Lord that even when we're not obedient, He still loves us, forgives us, is not angry with us, and has mercy upon us. We should be obedient to whatever God asks us to do, but when we fail, we need to praise our Savior because He never fails.

Mission

Be obedient the first time God asks you to do something. You never know the eternal consequences that may follow. Don't take Jesus for granted nor His mercy upon us.

Daily Notes: _____

_____

_____

_____

_____

_____

OPPORTUNITY

October 3

Opportunity: a situation or condition favorable for attainment of a goal.

> **Nahum 1:7** — *The Lord is good, a strong hold in the day of trouble; and he knoweth them that trust in him.*

Testimony

We have an opportunity to know Jesus right now. Jesus knows who knows Him and who doesn't. The Lord is good, and a strong hold for those in trouble and He knows them that trust in Him. Why wouldn't you want to trust in an all-knowing, loving, amazing Creator? You have an opportunity right now. You have an opportunity to know the Lord, tell others about Him, trust Him, and watch the amazing things He will do around you — in your life and in the lives of others. Take every opportunity to glorify the Lord.

My husband told me once after we were at an event, "I could really see you as a speaker." Later that night we had went on date and started talking about that. I said, "I could see myself doing it, too. How do you get started in something like that?" He replied, "You make an opportunity." So that is exactly what I did. I made a flyer and announced it on social networks that I would be speaking for the first time at my church. The theme was just say "Yes, Jesus!" to every opportunity you get. If you don't currently have an opportunity, then you create an opportunity for yourself. Jesus is worth every opportunity that comes your way. Not only that, but Jesus creates opportunities to be glorified.

Mission

Just say "Yes, Jesus" to every opportunity you get to glorify the Lord. He will bless you and the opportunity every time.

Daily Notes: _____

OUT

Out: away from, or not in, the normal or usual place, position, or state.

> **Habakkuk 3:19** — *The Lord God is my strength and he will make my feet like hinds feet, and he will make me to walk upon mine high places. To the chief singer on my stringed instruments.*

Testimony

Someone close to me shared a story with me. She felt like she just wanted to get out to have a little bit of time to herself. She has a busy life. She is an amazing wife, mother, teacher, author, and so many other things, but just wanted some time to herself. The feeling of wanting out turned into an "I just really need out," type feeling. Once she got out, she drove down the road, doing her own thing, spending time with herself getting her "out" time. She realized then that she was lonely, and didn't really need out at all. What she needed was within her the whole time. She needed to pray for peace and energy from her Savior. Jesus has what we need. We don't need to get "out" to find it. It's great to serve a living Savior who has what we need all the time, whether we're "in" or "out!"

Mission

Pray for strength from Jesus. He is the only one who knows what you need, and will set you up on high places, whether you're "in" or "out"!

Daily Notes: _____

_____

_____

ONE

One: being or amounting to a single unit or individual or entire thing, item, or object rather than two or more; a single.

> **1 Samuel 17:49** — *And David put his hand in his bag, and took thence a stone, and slang it, and smote the Philistine in his forehead, that the stone sunk into his forehead; and he fell upon his face to the Earth.*

Testimony

David picked up five stones, but it only took one. We might walk around with a bunch of plan B's, but Jesus has one plan for us — it's plan A, and it will not fail. Plan A was a stone. A stone in the hands of a person in the will of God is enough to take a giant down. When you're serving Jesus, make Him your plan A and you won't need a plan B or four other stones.

Mission

Make Jesus your plan A.

Daily Notes: _____

_____

_____

_____

_____

_____

_____

_____

_____

ODDS

Odds: more likely to occur than something else.

> **Hebrews 11:16** — *But now they desire a better country, that is, an heavenly: wherefore God is not ashamed to be called their God: for he hath prepared for them a city.*

Testimony

This scripture reminds me of an old country hymn "I Can't Feel at Home in this World Anymore." The song goes, "Lord you know I have no friend like You, if Heaven were not my home. Lord what would I do?" I think as Christians, the more we serve the Lord, the more we look forward to Heaven. Especially when we go through hurt, pain, and trails in this life, we look forward to Heaven — a place God has prepared for those that believe upon Him. During those trails, if we keep our focus upon Jesus, we will come out of those hardships saying, "What are the odds that it would go like this?" When Jesus' hand is upon your life, and you acknowledge Him in all your ways, He will direct your paths and the odds of everything showing the glory of God will happen.

When I first started writing this devotional book, I came up with the idea of making all the words start with the same letter as the month they were in. For January, June, and July, I wondered how would I ever be able to think of that many "J" words. What are the odds that I would call my aunt and we would start spitting out "J" words, one after another? They are not odds. Jesus is in control.

Mission

Give Jesus your odds, and let him turn them into solid promises and guidance for your life.

Daily Notes: _____

_____

_____

OLD

Old: far advanced in the years of ones or its life.

Isaiah 43:18 — *Remember ye not the former things, neither consider the things of old.*

Testimony

You were once lost in sin; then Jesus saved you, changed you, and gave you a new life. The old life is gone, as should your old sinful life and habits. No matter how old you are, when you're serving Jesus, He can use you because you are His, made for His glory. Satan will always try to tell you that you're too old, young, ugly, fat, skinny, messed up, abused, strange, good, or perfect. Satan will always give you a lie to keep you from doing the work of the Lord, so when satan tries, remind him to "get out of here in the name of Jesus, because I'm not considering the former things that are old! I am serving a living Savior, who is growing me up every day." No matter what your age, size, or ability is, when you're serving Jesus. He will use you for His glory.

Mission

Do not consider the things of old.

Daily Notes: _____

_____

_____

_____

_____

_____

_____

OCCUPIED

October 8

Occupied: to take or fill up

Nahum 1:1 — *The burden of Nineveh. The book of the vision of Nahum the Elkoshite.*

Testimony

Nahum was occupied with the doom of Nineveh. He cared for the people and he was giving them a warning of what was coming. He also told them about the Lord, and all the good that He did. What are you occupied with in your life? Take a self-inventory of what is taking up most of your time — that is what you are occupied with. If it's not the things of the Lord, then change what is occupying your time and spend some time with the Lord. In this world it's easy to get occupied with work and life. Time goes by fast and at the end of the day, how much time did we spend with the Lord? Let spending time with the Lord occupy your heart and soul to where it's a 'must' every day. Nahum was occupied with spreading the word. We should be also.

Mission

Be occupied with Jesus.

Daily Notes: _____

_____

_____

_____

_____

_____

_____

_____

OFFERING

Offering: something offered in worship or devotion.

> **Luke 7:37** — *And, behold a woman in the city, which was a sinner, when she knew that Jesus sat at meat in the Pharisees house, brought an alabaster box of ointment,*

Testimony

She boldly walked into where Jesus was, let down her hair [which was against her culture at the time] and wept as she washed his feet. She offered Jesus her best ointment, her hair, and herself. She was completely overwhelmed with His greatness. I imagine she poured the whole bottle out and didn't save any for herself. She offered all that she had to Jesus. Jesus said unto her, "Thy sins are forgiven. Thy faith hath saved thee. Go in peace." We are talking about a sinner here with many sins; but one meeting with Jesus and she is completely forgiven of all her sins after she dumped her whole self and ointment on Jesus. Jesus forgave all her sins. One act and she was forgiven of all she had ever done. When you offer your whole heart to Jesus, He cleanses you, forgives you of your sins, and makes you white as snow. Jesus gives us a clean slate, no matter how much sin you have done. Jesus is bigger than all of it.

Mission

Offer your whole heart to Jesus.

Daily Notes: _____

_____

_____

_____

_____

OUTLINE

October 10

Outline: the line by which a figure or object is defined or bounded

2 Timothy 4:2 — *Preach the word; be instant in season, and out of season; reprove, rebuke, exhort with all longsuffering and doctrine.*

Testimony

Outlining the Bible helps a person prepare and teach scripture in an easy, clear, and logical way. This scripture above is talking about not teaching or preaching to itching ears; basically, not telling people what they *want* to hear, but what they *need* to hear, the truth of the matter. My husband told me a story once about a man in his life that approached him in Godly wisdom and told him what he needed to hear. It wasn't necessarily what he wanted to hear at the time. Now many, many, years later, my husband still thinks about that and thanks God for that moment of honesty.

Mission

Speak with eternity in mind, not satisfying the moment.

Daily Notes: _____

_____

_____

_____

_____

_____

_____

_____

OF

Of: used to indicate derivation, origin, or source.

Galatians 3:26 — *For ye are all the children of God by faith in Christ Jesus.*

Testimony

You are a CHILD OF GOD. Have the faith to believe the truth that you belong to Jesus Christ. Refer to yourself, and today, call yourself a CHILD OF GOD because that is exactly who you are! We are no longer under the condemnation of the law, or a slave to sin, but we are free in Christ, made new, and accepted of Him.

Mission

Be confident of who you belong to.

Daily Notes: _____

_____

_____

_____

_____

_____

_____

_____

_____

_____

_____

_____

_____

OWED

October 12

Owed: to be in debt to

Luke 7:41 — *There was a certain creditor which had two debtors: the one owed five hundred pence, and the other fifty.*

Testimony

My husband got up at church to lead the service on this exact scripture. His wisdom blew me away as he spoke, breaking down this scripture. He said, "It's easier look at the one with the five hundred pence and feel sorry for them — the one that is clearly far away, living in sin, and at the point of almost begging for hope. It's easier to witness to them, forgive them, and lead them to the Lord. They might even be begging to hear it. What about the man with fifty? The man that has everything going right for him, receiving the praise of men, is the person that's going to be the hardest to witness to. They might not even know how much they truly need Jesus. We must witness to all of them — the man with the five hundred and the man with fifty." Overall, we can't let the world determine who needs Jesus the most. We must tell both of the men — the one with five hundred and the one with fifty — about Jesus, whether they think they need it or not. Everyone needs to know about Jesus. Souls are at stake.

Mission

Let everyone know about Jesus.

Daily Notes: _____

_____

_____

_____

OPEN

Open: not closed or barred at the time

> **Luke 24:2** — *And they found the stone rolled away from the sepulcher.*

Testimony

Can you imagine the emotions that must have overtaken them as they went to the sepulcher and it was open? The stone was rolled away! Jesus fulfilled the scriptures just as He said He would do. He said, "The Son of man must be delivered into the hands of sinful men, and be crucified, and the third day rise again." Jesus always does what He says He will do. He is Savior of the world and would do it all again just for you.

Mission

Rejoice! Rejoice! The stone was rolled away!

Daily Notes: _____

_____

_____

_____

_____

_____

_____

_____

_____

_____

OBTAIN

Obtain: to come into possession of; get, or acquire.

> **Daniel 4:33** — *The same hour was the thing fulfilled upon Nebuchadnezzar: and he was driven from men, and did eat grass as oxen, and his body was wet with the dew of heaven, till his hairs were grown like eagles feathers, and his nails like birds claws.*

Testimony

Daniel obtained many interpretations of King Nebuchadnezzar's dreams. However, when the King didn't obey the dream interpretations, he was taught a lesson in pride that eventually brought him to the point of praising the Lord. Nebuchadnezzar obtained the looks of a wild beast, acted like a beast and was driven from men. While this was going on, Nebuchadnezzar looked up, praised the Lord, and honored Him. At the end of this, Nebuchadnezzar states "praise and extol and honor the King of heaven, all whose works are truth, and his ways judgment: and those that walk in pride he is able to abase." Nebuchadnezzar obtained a lesson in pride the hard way. Let us learn from Nebuchadnezzar and not be prideful, but humbly serve the Lord and others.

Mission

Nebuchadnezzar obtained a lesson in pride. You don't want to learn the hard way. Be humble. Get rid of pride.

Daily Notes: _____

_____

_____

_____

ORDINARY

Ordinary: of no special quality or interest.

> **Philippians 2:8** — *And being found in fashion a man, he humbled himself, and became obedient unto death, even the death of the cross.*

Testimony

You are not just an ordinary person. Jesus Christ humbled himself in the fashion of a man, became obedient unto death — even the death of the cross — and died for you and me. Jesus didn't do all that for you to consider yourself just ordinary. You are absolutely extraordinary, made in the image of Christ. The plans He has for you, and the love He has for you would absolutely blow your mind. You are one of a kind. You were created by Jesus.

Mission

Know you're extraordinary, not ordinary.

Daily Notes: _____

_____

_____

_____

_____

_____

_____

_____

_____

_____

OFF

October 16

Off: so as to be no longer supported or attached.

> **Luke 17:17** — *And Jesus answering said, Were there not ten cleansed? But where are the nine?*

Testimony

Jesus healed ten lepers. Only one turned back when he noticed the disease was gone. With a loud voice, he glorified the Lord, fell down on his face at His feet, and thanked Him. All ten received a physically healing and noticed their disease was gone. Only one received a spiritual healing. His salvation was complete.

Mission

Once your prayers are answered, don't forget to praise the Lord. Fall down on your face, worship Him and thank Him for it!

Daily Notes: _____

_____

_____

_____

_____

_____

_____

_____

_____

_____

_____

_____

OTHER

Other: additional or further.

> **Judges 7:4** — *And the Lord said unto Gideon, The people are yet too many; bring them down unto the water, and I will try them for thee there: and it shall be, that of whom I say unto thee, This shall go with thee, the same shall go with thee, and of whosoever I say unto thee, This shall not go with thee, the same shall not go.*

Testimony

Gideon gathered too large of an army. God tried them and drastically downsized the army. Gideon's army went from thousands upon thousands to an army of three hundred men. What if Gideon would have stayed focused on the others? What if Gideon would not have obeyed God and focused on the ones leaving and being eliminated? Put yourself in Gideon's shoes. He just selected an army. Now he is being told by the Lord, "It's too big; let me eliminate." Gideon obeyed God, and wasn't focused on the all the thousands of others leaving. Instead he focused on the ones God picked to fight. God can do amazing things in small numbers. Don't focus on the things in your life that God has eliminated. He has eliminated that old life and past sins for a reason. He has eliminated it to take you further into where He wants you to be.

Mission

Don't focus on the "other things." Focus on the God things.

Daily Notes: _____

_____

_____

OFFENSE

Offense: a violation or breaking of a social or moral rule; transgression; sin.

> **Luke 17:1** — *Then said he unto the disciples, it is impossible but that offences will come: but woe unto him, through whom they come.*

Testimony

This is a reality: We *will* experience being offended and giving offense! The Word tells us not to give or take offence. So why, then, is it still a reality? This is something we have been warned about from Christ. Jesus knows we are not perfect; that's why we needed Him, a perfect Savior. He warns us that offences will come, not that they may, but they will. Jesus doesn't leave it at that. He warns us of the seriousness of taking it or giving it. He goes on to say that no matter what, when a brother or sister in Christ asks for forgiveness you are to forgive them, regardless of how many times they ask. Forgiveness isn't just for them either. It's for you as well. Jesus is serious about loving everyone, especially our brothers and sisters in Christ. Check yourself, your family, your church, and your social circle. Is there any offense? If so, put a stop to it. Don't partake in it. Show God's love and forgiveness, and move on.

Mission

True Christian fellowship with anyone has Christ in the center of it. Evaluate your relationships with everyone. If offense is involved, then put Christ in the center of it.

Daily Notes: _____

_____

OFFENDED

October 19

Offended: to irritate, annoy, or anger; cause resentful displeasure in.

> **2 Corinthians 6:3** — *Giving no offence in any thing, that the ministry be not blamed.*

Testimony

You're thinking, "How is it possible to live this life, in this world, with no offence ever being taken or given?" The only way it's possible is when Christ is in the center of our heart, our world, and our mind. Studying this and writing this, I feel my life changing. I had a lack of knowledge of how serious Jesus views offenses being given and taken. The Word actually states *give no offence in anything*. Now knowing and understanding how serious Jesus is on the issue, makes me want to change my life, starting today.

Change yours, too. Don't take part in the conversation that is involving someone that's not around to defend themselves. Don't laugh on someone's behalf. Don't listen to gossip or negative talk. Make changes to grow closer to the Lord. Make changes that will reflect that you're living your life according to the Word of God.

Mission

Pray this prayer. "Help me, Jesus, not to give offense or take it. Help me to not participate in negative talk or gossip, but to show the world You and Your Word. Help me to do this in every aspect of my life throughout every day." Amen.

Daily Notes: _____

_____

_____

_____

OBED

October 20

Obed: name means serving and worshipping. Obed is the son of Boaz and Ruth. The grandfather of David.

> **Ruth 4:16** — *And Naomi took the child, and laid it in her bosom, and became nurse unto it.*

Testimony

I'm sure, given Naomi's life history, there was a time in Naomi's life where she probably thought in her distress, "I'll never be a grandmother." Can you imagine losing your son and husband? Naomi changed her name at one point. We know that she was in distress, but here we see a beautiful picture at the end of the book of Ruth. Naomi, although Boaz isn't her son, takes Obed as her own, as her grandchild. We see how wonderful and good God is in redeeming bad circumstances. It didn't matter that Ruth wasn't technically her daughter, or Boaz her son. We see through Naomi's love for Ruth, and Ruth's love for Naomi, that they ultimately all had a happy ending. Jesus gives us that happy ending. Jesus gives us our heart's desires. Naomi was a grandmother after all.

Mission

Look beyond your circumstances.

Daily Notes: _____

_____

_____

_____

_____

_____

_____

OBED-EDOM

October 21

Obed-Edom: He was specially instructed the custody of the ark. It remained in his house for three months and his house was blessed.

> **1 Chronicles 13:12** — *And David was afraid of God that day, saying, How shall I bring the ark of God home to me?*

Testimony

Earlier in scripture, Uzza died from putting his hand forth to hold the ark when the oxen stumbled. As innocent as this act may have seemed, it went against God's law — that's why Uzza died. As a result of his death, David was afraid and left the ark inside Obed-Edom's house. Because of fear, David missed out on a blessing. Because of Uzza's disobedience, he died. The result of those two men's acts resulted in Obed-Edom being blessed. Everything he had was blessed, too. God can make good come from bad. Obed-Edom was blessed because he was willing and obedient.

Mission

Be willing and obedient.

Daily Notes: _____

_____

_____

_____

_____

_____

_____

_____

OATH

October 22

Oath: to witness ones determination to speak the truth. A statement or promise strengthened by such an appeal.

> **Matthew 5:34** — *But I say unto you, Swear not at all; neither by heaven; for it is Gods throne:*

Testimony

Jesus is teaching on oaths. The point He makes is: don't do it. Speak in such a way that your yes means yes, and your no means no. Let the oath you make before man always point to, lead back to, and uplift Jesus Christ. Living this way by controlling your mouth and thoughts will help defuse a lot of turmoil around you. If people look at you and wonder what you stand for, then apparently you have been compromising a bit in your life.

Mission

Let your yes mean yes, and your no mean no!

Daily Notes: _____

_____

_____

_____

_____

_____

_____

_____

_____

_____

OBEY

October 23

Obey: to comply with or follow the commands, restrictions, wishes, or instructions of.

> **Matthew 5:44** — *But I say unto you, Love your enemies, bless them that curse you, do good to them that hate you, and pray for them which despitefully use you, and persecute you;*

Testimony

We are to obey all of God's Word, but what about this verse? Really? How is that even possible? The only way it is possible is with the prayer, guidance, and your heart being sold out to Jesus. If we are supposed to love our enemies, how much more should we love our families, friends, and church? If we're supposed to do good to them that hate us, then how much more good are we supposed to do to them that love us? Jesus is serious about loving people and doing good to all. If you have found yourself being a hater, it's probably because you're focusing on yourself and your feelings. Let Jesus fight your battles and defend you. Don't compromise who you are. Just live your life according to the Word and let Jesus take care of the rest.

Mission

Don't be a hater. Just obey.

Daily Notes: _____

_____

_____

_____

_____

OBJECTION

October 24

Objection: a reason or argument offered in disagreement, opposition, refusal, or disapproval.

> **Matthew 9:9** — *And as Jesus passed forth from thence, he saw a man, named Matthew, sitting at the receipt of custom: and he saith unto him, Follow me. And he arose, and followed him.*

Testimony

Matthew didn't object Jesus when Jesus told him "follow me." Matthew didn't complain or say, "Let me take care of this first... Hold on, I'm almost finished with my task here...Let me go say goodbye to my loved ones and friends...I need to go back and get a few things." Matthew just arose and followed him.

Scripture doesn't tell us what Matthew was doing. Scripture just says that he went. What are we doing when Jesus calls us to do something or to follow him? Are we making excuses, going back for things or finishing what we're doing? Or are we trusting that Jesus is bigger than all of that and has a plan? Whatever you're doing when Jesus calls you to do something or to follow him, you can trust that whatever it is, it isn't as important as what Jesus wants for you.

Mission

Trust and go. Do not object.

Daily Notes: _____

_____

_____

_____

_____

OX

Ox: used as a draft animal.

1 Timothy 5:18 — *For the scripture saith, Thou shalt not muzzle the ox that treadeth out the corn. And, The labourer is worthy of his reward.*

Testimony

The ox did not have a muzzle on so he could freely eat the corn that he was helping to obtain. The same is true for us. What we are laboring we will be rewarded for. The same with our preacher, deacons, and those that make the decisions of the church. The gospel they preach will also "feed" them and help them in their daily life. When you're in church or hearing the gospel elsewhere, are you listening with a muzzle on? Or are you listening with the muzzle off? Take the muzzle off so you can enjoy it and it can take root in your heart. When eating food, we don't just swallow it. We put it in our mouth, chew it, enjoy it, and then swallow it. The same is to be said of the Word of God. Take the muzzle off and let it take root. Chew on it a bit. Think about the words that are being spoken and enjoy your reward. Jesus and His blessings are your reward.

Mission

Take the muzzle off and enjoy the gospel. If the ox didn't wear it, you don't need to either.

Daily Notes: _____

_____

_____

_____

_____

O'CLOCK

October 26

O'clock: of, by or according to the clock.

John 13:38 — *Jesus answered him, "Wilt thou lay down thy life for my sake? Verily, verily, I say unto thee, The cock shall not crow, till thou hast denied me thrice.*

Testimony

Jesus knew Peter would deny him. At the time when Jesus is saying this, Peter probably thought in his mind, "I never will." Then the time came. They took Jesus, and Peter was probably scared. Peter had his chance and people started noticing him. They asked, "Aren't you the one we saw with Jesus? Don't you follow him? Wasn't it you in the garden?" Three times, just like Jesus said he would do. Peter denied Christ, and the cock crowed.

Can you imagine the feelings that over came Peter after he denied Christ and the cock crowed? He probably thought he could get by with denying Him. Jesus isn't right here. Can you imagine hearing that predicted sound when the cock crowed? The time that he was warned about had come. We are warned now that we need to be ready for Jesus coming back. We are warned that He will come back. So are we ready? First accept Christ as your Savior and make Heaven your eternal home. Second, start spreading the gospel so others can know Him, too. Be prepared. Be ready. Don't let the cock crow and catch you.

Mission

Don't check the clock. Now is the time. Accept Jesus and spread the Gospel.

Daily Notes: _____

_____

OAK

Oak: hard, durable wood of such a tree.

Luke 6:43 — *For a good tree bringeth not forth corrupt fruit; neither doth a corrupt tree bring forth good fruit.*

Testimony

What kind of fruit are we bearing? What kind of tree are you? If you were a tree, what would you look like? Would you be a strong oak? Or would you be a dead log? The fruit you're bearing can be a good indication of what's going on in your life. If you have drama and not peace, what are you putting out there for others to take? Jesus promises us peace, a sound mind, and love. Let's demonstrate that so we can have that in our lives. Imagine a dead tree with no leaves. Now imagine living your life with everything you give and do for Jesus. He keeps adding life to that tree — green, lush, living leaves.

Keep pressing on, no matter what dead things are happening in your life, keep adding life to your tree. I promise, you will get to the point where you have become a strong oak with Jesus. Jesus doesn't leave things dead; he raises the dead and brings the dead back to life. He can do that for you, too. Keep adding life, love, and peace to yourself, others, and your situations. Before too long you won't feel like a dead log. Instead, you will feel like a strong oak tree.

Mission

Be an oak.

Daily Notes: _____

_____

_____

OBJECT

Object: anything that is visible or tangible and is relatively stable in form.

> **John 20:29** — *Jesus saith unto him, Thomas, because thou hast seen me, thou hast believed: blessed are they that have not seen, and yet have believed.*

Testimony

Thomas wanted to see the object. Thomas wanted to see the nails. Thomas wanted to reach out and touch the side of Jesus before he could believe. Thomas needed proof, but Jesus said, "blessed are those who have not seen, and yet they believe." It's called faith. Faith that Jesus is who He says He is, will keep the promise's He has made, and will do the things He says He is going to do. You must have faith. Don't let an object get in your way for you clearly seeing Jesus.

Mission

Remove all objects so you can faithfully see clearly.

Daily Notes: _____

_____

_____

_____

_____

_____

_____

_____

OBLIVION

October 29

Oblivion: the state of being completely forgotten or unknown.

John 3:16 — *For God so loved the world, that he gave his only begotten Son, that whosoever believeth in him should not perish, but have everlasting life.*

Testimony

You never have to worry about being in a state of oblivion with Jesus, as long as you are living. He will never forget you. You are so loved, thought of, and cared about by our Savior. He created you and loves you. The last thing He will ever do is put you in a state of oblivion. He will never do that as long as we're living and have accepted Him. How often have we put Jesus in a state of oblivion? How often have we acted like Jesus isn't around? Truth is, Jesus will never do that to us, so we should never do that to Him. Keep Jesus constantly on your mind. Keep the love He has for you and others constantly on your mind as well.

Mission

Don't put your Savior in an oblivion state. Instead, make Him known, and remember Him every second of every day.

Daily Notes: _____

_____

_____

_____

_____

_____

_____

OBSESSION

October 30

Obsession: the domination of ones thoughts or feelings by a persistent idea, image, or desire.

> **Philippians 4:8** — *Finally, brethren, whatsoever things are true, whatsoever things are honest, whatsoever things are pure, whatsoever things are lovely, whatsoever things are of good report; if there be any virtue, and if there be any praise, think on these things.*

Testimony

What is your obsession? If you don't know, then what do you do or think about most often? That's what your obsession is. If you're thinking thoughts that are against God's Word — negative, or unpleasant — remind yourself of this verse and use this verse to consider if what you're thinking is right. If it's not honest, pure, lovely, good, or worthy of praise, then get rid of those thoughts, feelings, emotions, or lifestyles.

Mission

Use this verse as a checklist to live by. Control your emotions and thoughts so that what you're thinking and doing is lining up with God's Word. It will bring you peace. As soon as a negative thought comes, get out your checklist and ask yourself: Is this true? Is this honest? You probably won't make it through the list before you have to get rid of it.

Daily Notes: _____

_____

_____

_____

_____

OCTOBER

October 31

Reflection of the month of October:

Philippians 4:7 — *And the peace of God, which passeth all understanding, shall keep your hearts and minds through Christ Jesus.*

Testimony

Look back at this month. Have you grown in Jesus this month? If you haven't done this already, then give your heart and mind back to Jesus so you will grow. Let Him give you peace that passes all understanding. Do you have peace? If not, then give your heart and mind back to Jesus and let Him give you peace. Start your day off by giving Jesus control. He will keep your heart and mind at peace. That will allow you to grow!

Mission

I encourage you to look back this month to the moments you have had peace, and thank Jesus for giving you that peace. Looking forward, give your heart and mind to Jesus so that you will continue to have that peace, and thank Him for it.

Daily Notes: _____

_____

_____

_____

_____

_____

_____

_____

_____

NEEDS

November 1

Needs: a necessity

Matthew 6:28 — *And why take ye thought for raiment? Consider the lilies of the field, how they grow; they toil not, neither do they spin:*

Testimony

In earlier verses in this chapter, Jesus talked about the birds; now he is talking about the lilies. Jesus states, "How much more precious are you then they?" Jesus takes care of the birds of the air and the lilies of the field. Don't you think He will take care of you? He takes care of every creature. You are His masterpiece. He didn't create you to leave you. He created you for His glory. Jesus will meet your needs above and beyond what you think you need at the moment. Jesus is not only taking care of your needs now, He is taking care of your needs until the end of your life.

Mission

Don't worry.

Daily Notes: _____

_____

_____

_____

_____

_____

_____

_____

_____

NEAR

November 2

Near: close to a point or place not far away.

> **Matthew 24:42** — *Watch therefore: for ye know not what hour your Lord doth come.*

Testimony

Is the coming of the Lord near? Nobody knows. We're told to watch as if it is; to watch daily as if it is near; to watch hourly, down to the minute as if it's that close. The Lord uses the word hour in this verse to remind us to watch. Exactly what do we watch for? Watch for the coming of the Lord. Watch and make sure you're ready, your loved ones and friends around you are ready, and that what you're doing is lining up with the Word. What do you want to be caught doing when the Lord comes back?

Mission

Keep it near in your minds.

Daily Notes: _____

_____

_____

_____

_____

_____

_____

_____

_____

_____

NAP

Nap: to sleep for a short time.

Acts 12:6 — *And when Herod would have brought him forth, the same night Peter was sleeping between two soldiers, bound with two chains: and the keepers before the door kept the prison.*

Testimony

Peter wasn't taking a nap! Peter was sleeping! If I was Peter and in that situation, I think the last thing I would be able to do is sleep. *We're talking about your death the next day, Peter! You're not getting a cup of coffee or pancakes in the morning. You're getting your head on a platter by Herod!* But Peter was sleeping! Sleeping! He was sleeping with two soldiers by his side, as well as being bound with chains. This is the kind of peace that is only possible through Jesus. Peter slept the night before his death sentence, bound in chains, with soldiers around him. You can find peace in your situation, too. Peter turned to Jesus and an angel of the Lord had to actually shake Peter and wake him up. How amazing is that? The angel shakes him, awakes him, and then Peter walks out. Turn to Jesus and receive the peace He gives. Let Jesus break your chains and walk out of the darkness like Peter did!

Mission

Let Jesus break your chains, then walk out of your prison like Peter.

Daily Notes: _____

_____

_____

_____

NOT

November 4

Not: used to express negation, denial, refusal, or prohibition.

Genesis 3:4 — *And the serpent said unto the woman, Ye shall not surely die:*

Testimony

The word "not" — a three-letter word — caused the fall of mankind. How important are the words we speak or listen to? The words Eve choose to listen to the day in the garden caused sin to enter into the world and the fall of man. If the serpent had spoken the truth and said, "You will surely die," Eve most likely wouldn't have eaten the fruit. You wouldn't take something if someone told you, "If you eat this you will die." But one word changed the whole outcome of the situation. One word got thoughts and emotions rolling. Watch carefully the words you speak, but also be aware of what you listen to. One word can change your life. One word, in this case, changed all of our lives and the world forever.

Mission

Be careful what you listen to.

Daily Notes: _____

_____

_____

_____

_____

_____

_____

_____

NAME

Name: a word or combination of words by which a person, place, or thing, a body or class, or any object of thought is designated, called, or known.

> **Ruth 1:14** — *And they lifted up their voice, and wept again: and Orpah kissed her mother in law but, Ruth clave unto her.*

Testimony

Biblical names often are full of rich meaning. The names of people in the Bible often went right along with what they accomplished or did in their life. That tells us something very important. It tells us that our names are important. What we choose to name our children is important. And what we name situations and ourselves is crucial. In this story of Ruth, Naomi actually changed her name based on her circumstances. However, Ruth and Orpah keep their names. The meaning of their names showed their character. Ruth's name means friend. Her name shows her character to the fullest. Ruth was the most wonderful friend Naomi could have. She was much more than a friend. Orpah means 'back of the neck,' which is all Naomi saw of Orpah when she turned back and left Naomi and Ruth. When you're studying and reading the word, dig into the meaning of Biblical names. They often help you understand what you're reading. More importantly, pay attention to what you name things. Naomi renamed her situation for the worse. Make sure when you're naming things; use names that line up with the Word of God.

Mission

You have the right to name your situation based on what God can do, not what you can do. —Pastor Steven Furtick

Embrace the name you have. You are a child of God.

Daily Notes: _____

NATURE

November 6

Nature: the material world, especially, surrounding humankind and existing independently of human activities.

> **Psalm 89:11** — *The heavens are thine, the earth also is thine: as for the world and the fullness thereof, thou hast founded them.*

Testimony

God has created everything in nature. I heard a preacher once say, "The problem with Christians is that we're living like God is small. Look at the stars, everything in nature, the wings of birds, and gravity. All this was created by God for His glory. Jesus has founded all of this." Why do we live and act like He is small? The next time we're faced with something bigger than we are, let's remind ourselves of how big our Savior is.

Mission

Look at the stars.

Daily Notes: _____

_____

_____

_____

_____

_____

_____

_____

_____

NEHEMIAH

November 7

Nehemiah: a book of the bible bearing his name.

Nehemiah 2:2 — *Wherefore the king said unto me, why is thy countenance sad, seeing thou art not sick? This is nothing else but sorrow of heart. Then I was very sore afraid.*

Testimony

Nehemiah had a journey before he built the wall. The journey began with prayer for repentance, a broken heart, fear, and anxiety. Then he started to see God's plan come together. The king said unto him, "I can see your heart is full of sorrow." Nehemiah had a sorrowful heart before he embraced God's plan. Sometimes our broken heart is preparing us for the solid promises from the Lord.

Mission

Embrace.

Daily Notes: _____

_____

_____

_____

_____

_____

_____

_____

_____

_____

NEVERTHELESS

November 8

Nevertheless: however; in spite of that.

Nehemiah 4:9 — Nevertheless we made out prayer unto our God, and set a watch against them day and night, because of them.

Testimony

Nehemiah had adversaries that were conspiring against him. Nevertheless, he prayed, but he didn't stop there. He put action with his prayers and did what he could. He armed his workers and reminded them not to be afraid because the Lord was with them. Fear and threat didn't hinder Nehemiah from rebuilding the wall. Instead, it helped push them to get it done — in God's speed. Don't let the threats or fears that others speak over you hinder you from doing God's work. Be reminded of Nehemiah's words of "nevertheless." Pray about it and go on. Let it help you get the job done whether you receive criticism or praise. Remember that you're working unto the Lord and not men.

Mission

Nevertheless, just pray. Then know it's taken care of so move on.

Daily Notes: _____

_____

_____

_____

_____

_____

_____

NABAL

November 9

Nabal: a wealthy Calebite, husband of Abigail, who refused rightful tribute to King David for protecting his flocks.

> **1 Samuel 25:10** — *And Nabal answered David's servants, and said, Who is David? And who is the son of Jesse? There be many servants now a days that break away every man from his master.*

Testimony

Nabal refused David's request. Not only did Nabal refuse David's request, but he also didn't acknowledge David or his servants. On top of that, he was rude and unkind. David's reaction was anger towards Nabal. Destruction was ready to come upon his family but Abigail, Nabel's wife, came up with a plan [in all her great wisdom] that pacified David's anger. Although this was a bad situation, God made good come from it. Because of this meeting, David was able to meet Abigail. Once Nebal had died, Abigail became David's wife. God has a way of making good come out of bad situations. I'm sure David and Abigail never forgot the circumstances of their first meeting, but nevertheless, they met. Don't be a fool, like Nabal, by creating problems for yourself and others. Instead, be wise like Abigail. Let Jesus make a provision for the problems you face. What was once a problem for Abigail, with Jesus, it then turned into a promise and then a provision for Abigail's life.

Mission

Give your problems to Jesus, and hang on to God's promises. Then watch a provision come from it.

Daily Notes: _____

_____

NICODEMUS

November 10

Nicodemus: a secret follower of Jesus.

> **John 3:9** — *Nicodemus answered and said unto him, How can these things be?*

Testimony

Nicodemus was talking to Jesus. Jesus was telling him how a man could be born again — not physically, but spiritually. At this point when Nicodemus came to Jesus, he was a secret follower, but there is no evidence of a changed life in him. The changes in a converted person's life should be like the wind; we should be able to see and feel it. It isn't until later in John chapter seven that Nicodemus starts to change, his walk with Christ gets bolder, as he stands, becoming His disciple. If you are living for Jesus, there has to be a change made in you — one of such magnitude that people look at you and see a completely different person. People need to see a new man. You need to look more like Jesus and less like you.

Mission

Make the change.

Daily Notes: _____

_____

_____

_____

_____

_____

_____

NINEVEH

November 11

Nineveh: the ancient capital of Assyria.

> **Jonah 1:2** — *Arise, go to Nineveh, that great city, and cry against it; for their wickedness is come up before me.*

Testimony

Don't run away from where God wants you to go. It doesn't work. Being out of God's will only causes turmoil, sadness, and distress. Jonah ran away from God. The result was a storm, and consumption by a giant fish for three days. Where did the fish spit him out? It was upon dry land, but not right at Nineveh. He still had to journey there. Why wouldn't God just let the fish spit Jonah out as close as he could to Nineveh? Scripture doesn't say, but I would assume it was because God wanted to see if Jonah would be willing to preach and do what He wanted him to do. Who knows what happened during that journey to Nineveh. Jonah might have spent most of the journey in prayer before he got there to preach. Jonah had to stay focused on the mission during that journey. The mission was to preach and spread the gospel when he arrived at Nineveh.

Mission

Stay focused on your mission from the Lord. No matter how long the journey is, stay focused on Jesus.

Daily Notes: _____

_____

_____

_____

_____

NAOMI

Naomi: a female name: from a Hebrew word meaning "pleasant."

> **Proverbs 16:28** — *A forward man soweth strife: and a whisper separateth chief friends.*

Testimony

My husband and I had a life-changing trip to Florida once. One of the friends we met was a girl named Naomi. Her name means "pleasant" and that is exactly how she was. Meeting her changed our lives in one moment. We were in a small crowd when someone made fun of someone else in a joking like manner. I laughed and didn't think twice about it. Naomi said, "That person is not here to defend themselves. This makes me feel bad. I won't even listen or participate." She said all that in such a loving way that the other person didn't get offended. Instead, she apologized saying, "I didn't even realize that I was saying that." That moment made us look at our own social circle back home and realize we needed to do things differently. It's not even OK to listen or laugh; that's still participating. Nothing unkind should come out of our mouth. Everything we speak should glorify the Lord. That reminder and refresher from Naomi changed our lives. It makes us realize that area of our life needed to represent Christ better. I am forever thankful for that moment.

Mission

Think before you speak.

Daily Notes: _____

_____

_____

_____

NAOMI

November 13

Naomi: the mother-in-law of Ruth and the great-grandmother of David.

> **Ruth 3:11** — *And now, my daughter, fear not; I will do to thee all that thou requires: for all the city of my people doth know that thou art a virtuous woman.*

Testimony

How encouraging was Naomi to Ruth? Naomi told her to "fear not", and calls her a virtuous woman. Sometimes we need encouragement. In this moment, that was exactly what Ruth needed. Naomi gave Ruth the comfort she was seeking. Later Ruth returned to Naomi to let her know what she had done for Boaz. We need to provide people with encouragement, and sometimes just listen. Naomi and Ruth were each other's support. Who is your support? Who do you run to for advice or for a listening ear? Make sure the person you go to will lead you towards to Lord and will give you Godly wisdom, not worldly advice.

Mission

Encourage people in the Lord.

Daily Notes: _____

_____

_____

_____

_____

_____

_____

NAAMAN

November 14

Naaman: Hebrew name meaning "pleasantness."

2 Kings 5:1 — *Now Naaman, captain of the host of the king of Syria, was a great man with his master, and honourable, because by him the Lord had given deliverance unto Syria: he was also a mighty man in valour, but he was a leper.*

Testimony

Naaman actually means "pleasantness," but he was a leper. Naaman went to Elisha and went away in rage because he thought his healing should come to him differently. After speaking to his servants, Naaman finally gave in to what the prophet Elisha said and, as a result, he was healed. Are you postponing your healing because you're expecting it to come in a different way than what God has planned? Let Naaman's story be a reminder that God's answers are not always how we think they should be. If God tells you to do something seven times, don't stop the sixth time. Naaman washed himself in the river seven times then he was healed of the leprosy. Don't stop on the sixth dip.

Mission

Seek God and His healing for your life. Don't go off your expectations.

Daily Notes: _____

_____

_____

_____

_____

_____

NOAH

Noah: the patriarch who built a ship, in which he, his family, and animals of every species survived the Flood.

> **Genesis 9:3** — *Every moving thing that liveth shall be meat for you; even as the green herb have I given you all things.*

Testimony

After the flood, God told Noah, "Everything that moves is meat for you, and I have given you all things." God wants us to enjoy life. This verse is a reminder that Jesus wants us to enjoy food and all that we eat. He has given us this blessing. Jesus would not withhold anything good from His children. Noah could now eat the animals. God knew, when creating Noah, what would need to happen to sustain Noah's life. Not only did God know what Noah needed to survive, He wanted him to enjoy it!

God not only provides for us spiritually, but physically as well. Pray over your food and thank God for His creation for you to enjoy. Food is a blessing and a gift from God. It is a necessity to life; God gave it to us and wants us to enjoy it.

Mission

Start today, before your next meal, and bless your food before you eat it. Give thanks from where it came from.

Daily Notes: _____

_____

_____

_____

_____

_____

NAHUM

Nahum: a book of the bible bearing his name.

> **Nahum 1:1** — *The burden of Nineveh. The book of the vision of Nahum the Elkoshite.*

Testimony

Nahum is a book of lyric poetry of the highest quality. God used Nahum's skills to write a book of the Bible, deliver a message, and give comfort. Whatever your skill is, God will equip you to spread the gospel and use your skills to build up His Kingdom, just like He did for Nahum. Nahum used his skills to glorify the Lord while writing this book of the Old Testament. What are some of your skills? Think of ways you can use these skills to glorify God.

Mission

Let God use you and the skills He has equipped you with.

Daily Notes: _____

_____

_____

_____

_____

_____

_____

_____

_____

_____

_____

NATIONS

Nations: a large body of people, associated with a particular territory.

> **Psalm 33:12** — *Blessed is the nation whose God is the Lord; and the people whom he hath chosen for his own inheritance.*

Testimony

A nation that looks towards God will be blessed. Our nation was founded on Christian beliefs. Over time they keep getting compromised. If the law of the land changes and keeps straying further from God's Word, then take a step back and remember what your roots are. This nation was founded on God's Word. Let's remind people that God is still in control. Let's remind people of the past; let's not put God in the past, but put God in the future. Pray about every decision. Pray for our leaders, our country, and Israel. Pray for whom to vote for. Make sure your decisions that affect the nation are lined up with God's Word.

Mission

Don't forget the principles our nation was originally founded upon.

Daily Notes: _____

_____ _____

_____

_____

_____

_____

_____

NEWBORN

November 18

Newborn: recently or only just born.

> **Luke 2:7** — *And she brought forth her first born son, and wrapped him in swaddling clothes, and laid him in a manger; because there was no room for them in the inn.*

Testimony

A newborn baby to save the world? A baby in a manger to save the world? A baby from God, born unto a virgin, to cover the sins of the world? His name was Jesus! That baby, born unto Mary and Joseph, is the Savior of the world. The swaddling clothes she wrapped Him in not only protected His limbs to grow correctly, but was also a sign unto all that He was the Son of God *wrapped in swaddling clothes, and laying in a manger.* There were angels singing, "Glory to God in the highest, and on earth peace, goodwill towards men." That baby that was born unto Mary is still alive today just as much as He was the day He was born. Our Savior lives! He still lives today and is still saving the souls of men. Jesus was born so that one day He would lay down His life for us, and raise it back up and we could live in Him. He lived every day so we could know how to live according to His Word — spending Eternity with Him. Jesus' birth, the life He lived, and His death and resurrection is all for us. With His life, He glorified His Father.

Mission

Remember, Jesus is with you. He is alive! Everything He did was for you.

Daily Notes: _____

_____

_____

NECESSARY

November 19

Necessary: being essential

John 3:4 — *Nicodemus saith unto him, how can a man be born when he is old? Can he enter the second time into his mother's womb, and be born?*

Testimony

Nicodemus probably wondered, "is this being born again stuff really necessary?" With the comments Nicodemus made, its clear he was quite confused. Jesus talked to Nicodemus about a spiritual birth, which is necessary for eternal life — not born of the physical flesh, but born of the spirit. A spiritual birth takes place when you accept Christ as your Savior. This is the point in time where you are born of the spirit, you call upon the name of the Lord to enter into your heart and save you from hell. We all have had a necessary physical birth. It's even more important to have a spiritual birth so we can enter into the kingdom of Heaven.

Mission

Make sure you have had a spiritual birth. If you haven't, then now is your time. Accept Christ as your Savior. Call upon Him to enter into your heart and forgive you of your sins so you can live for Him from this day forth. It is necessary. If you have already accepted Christ, then think back to that day and time and thank God for calling you with His deep love for you into a personal relationship with Him. Focus on that personal relationship today. Thank Christ for saving you. It is necessary.

Daily Notes: _____

_____

_____

NOW

Now: at the present time or moment.

> **Isaiah 55:11** — *So shall my word be that goeth forth out of my mouth: it shall not return unto me void, but it shall accomplish that which I please, and it shall prosper in the thing whereto I sent it.*

Testimony

Now is the time to spread the Word. God commands us to do that, but here He gives us the blessed assurance that His Word will accomplish His purposes, and never come back unto us void. At times, when we're spreading the gospel the conversation or situation may get awkward and uncomfortable. When we have a very discouraging reaction, set your mind on making an eternal difference rather than making an earthly difference. No matter how your situation goes, it will never return void. At some point in that person's life, it will make a difference. If the difference is only eternal, it is worth it!

Mission

Don't focus on now. Focus on eternity.

Daily Notes: _____

_____

_____

_____

_____

_____

_____

_____

NEGLECT

November 21

Neglect: to pay no attention to

Genesis 19:15 — *And when the morning arose then the angles hastened Lot, saying, Arise, take thy wife, and thy two daughters, which are here; lest thou be consumed in the iniquity of the city.*

Testimony

Lot's story is a very disturbing one. If a person just picked up the Bible to read it — and this was the first thing they read —I bet they would be pretty confused. So why is this story in the Bible? What is the purpose of this very disturbing story? It was never God's purpose or intention for Lot to do the things that he did. God had big plans to prosper Lot, but Lot took matters into his own hands and allowed his soul to be vexed and greatly influenced by the unrighteousness of the city. We can learn from Lot's story how very disturbing and devastating life can be without God in it. Can you remember your life when you neglected God before you were saved? Ignoring God and taking matters into your own hands results in darkness and sin. We can learn from this story not to take matters into our own hands, neglecting the Lord's plans. Life without God is a life not worth living.

Mission

Don't neglect God's plans for you. They are better than yours.

Daily Notes: _____

_____

_____

_____

_____

NOTE

November 22

Note: a brief record of facts, topics, or thoughts, written down as an aid to memory.

> **Exodus 2:5** — *the daughter of Pharaoh came down to wash herself at the river; and her maidens walked along by the river's side; and when she saw the ark among the flags, she sent her maid to fetch it.*

Testimony

How much faith did Moses' mother have? She had enough faith to send her beloved baby down the river in a basket. She let him go and had no control over the outcome. God moved on the heart of Pharaoh's daughter when she found Moses in the basket. The daughter called for a woman to nurse the child, who was Moses' mother! Moses, because of the faith of his mother, escaped the fate of most Hebrew male infants. Our actions affect those around us. Moses' mother's action affected his life. Take note of your actions.

Mission

Note the faith of people in your Word. Let it build upon your own faith.

Daily Notes: _____ . _____

_____

_____

_____

_____

_____

NICHE

November 23

Niche: a place or position suitable or appropriate for a person or thing.

Hebrews 10:25 — *Not forsaking the assembling of ourselves together as the manner of some is; but exhorting one another: and so much the more, as ye see the day approaching.*

Testimony

You might feel like church is not really your niche; it's not where you fit in, or feel accepted. But church — wherever you attend — *is* your niche. It's where you belong, because Jesus made you worthy. Satan gives us every reason to feel as if church is not our niche. Don't be fooled by the lies of satan and the insecurities he is trying to make you carry. Church is the Lord's house. He is the One in charge. The church was established for you to grow, worship, and fellowship with Him.

The biggest lie satan gave me when I first started attending church was that I fit in better with the people at the bar. Satan had my mind focused on people and whatever else he could. As long as my mind was off Christ, that is what he wanted. Get to the point with church that it's not about you and how you feel about church; it's all about Jesus. You're going to church for Jesus. You're testifying for Jesus.

Mission

Everything you do; do it for Christ. It's your niche because He is living inside of you.

Daily Notes: _____
_____

NEVER-ENDING

Never-Ending: having no end

Hebrews 10:14 — *For by one offering he hath perfected forever them that are sanctified.*

Testimony

His love for you is never-ending. His sacrifice for you is never-ending. His promises and blessings for you are never-ending. Eternity is never-ending. Nothing about Jesus is temporary, but rather everything about Jesus is never-ending. We cannot even comprehend His sacrifice, love, or the blessings He has for us. Pray today that you can feel His never-ending love. Maybe you haven't felt loved, or maybe you're having a rough day, or maybe the exact opposite is happening — maybe everything is going great. So pray for His blessings to continue to flow. Praise God today no matter where you are. Praise Him right now. If it's hurt you're going through, Jesus' love is never-ending and bigger than that hurt. If its joy you're feeling, thank God and pray for the promises and the never-ending blessings to keep coming from Him.

Jesus is never-ending.

Mission

Pray for Jesus to give you a hug, wrapped in his never-ending love for you today.

Daily Notes: _____

_____

_____

_____

_____

NOON

November 25

Noon: midday

> **John 4:6** — *Now Jacobs well was there. Jesus therefore, being wearied with his journey, sat thus on the well: and it was about the sixth hour.*

Testimony

The woman went to the well when nobody else was there. The woman was embarrassed and ashamed, so she went alone. The woman had been living an unclean, sinful life, but Jesus would walk to the well for her. When others ran away from her, Jesus ran to her. Jesus will meet you at your well [in this case it was noon] anytime and anywhere. Jesus called me and continued to call me into a relationship with Him when I was running to the bars. Jesus will meet you where you are. Jesus met this woman at the well when it wasn't the typical time for drawling water. She didn't just leave with water that day; she left with living water and had the type of spiritual change where she would never thirst again. She met Jesus.

Mission

Met Jesus at your well and let him heal you with His Holiness.

Daily Notes: _____

_____

_____

_____

_____

_____

_____

NAILS

Nails: slender, rod shaped, piece of metal.

John 20:25 — *The other disciples therefore said unto him, We have seen the Lord. But he said unto them, Except I shall see in his hands the print of the nails, and put my finger into the print of the nails, and thrust my hand into his side, I will not believe.*

Testimony

Thomas needed to see and put his hand where the nails had been, to believe. Jesus let Thomas feel Him and see for himself, then Thomas believed. Jesus goes on to say, "Blessed are those who believe and have not seen." We all give Thomas a bad name. He is known as the doubter; but have you been there? I have.

A few years after I had been saved, I was sitting in church one day and started to doubt my salvation. I started to doubt, and ran out of fear, to the altar to pray a rededication prayer. I knew satan made me doubt. The next day, I was supposed to read a huge poem assignment for a college class, and I didn't read it. When I got to class, I felt so bad about what happened in church the night before. I opened my book and the first poem I read introduced me to 'doubter Thomas.' When I got in my car, I turned on the radio, and heard a song about Thomas. Then my mother called me and asked, "Have you ever heard of Thomas?" It got to the point where I said, "OK, Lord! I hear you. I was being a Thomas, but thank You so much for loving me and giving me that comfort." Jesus knows and understands us. Jesus comforted me that day, letting me know I wasn't alone. He was with me, just like He let Thomas know He was with him.

Mission

When you doubt, remember Thomas. Remember that Jesus is always here and He is who He says He is.

Daily Notes: _____

NAZARETH

November 27

Nazareth: a town in Israel. The childhood home of Jesus.

Luke 1:26 — *And in the sixth month the angel Gabriel was sent from God unto a city of Galilee, named Nazareth*

Testimony

Mary meets with an angel that tells her she will conceive the Son of God. At first Mary is confused "How will this happen?" I'm sure Mary, for an instant, experiences fear and confusion, but God didn't make a mistake when he picked Mary. He knew what the end result would be. Mary may have experienced fear and had questions, which we all would in that circumstance, but later we see Mary praising God with a joyful song. We see her testifying of God's greatness. While praising His name for doing great things in her, Mary states that her soul magnifies the Lord. Mary is a woman of God, favored among other women. Just like God choose Mary to deliver the Savior to the world, God has chosen you, too. God has picked you and put his Holy Spirit inside of you. You may not be carrying a baby like Mary, but you are carrying Jesus in your heart, soul, and spirit. The Holy Spirit lives inside of you. If you will acknowledge Jesus and stir that Spirit up, He will lead and guide you, just like He did Mary, every step of the way.

Mission

Jesus lives inside of you. Stir up the Spirit today.

Daily Notes: _____

_____

_____

_____

_____

NARROW

November 28

Narrow: not broad or wide

> **Matthew 7:14** — *Because strait is the gate, and narrow is the way, which leadeth unto life, and few there be that find it.*

Testimony

Jesus will enable you to find the narrow gate. You can't do it on your own. You can't do anything on your own. Jesus will call you. He is with you, but you must choose to go that way. Now in the world, it's time for Christians to be bolder than ever. You can look around and almost tell instantly who is serving Christ or not, and what areas are yielded to Christ or not. The world has much destruction; it's broad and wide. If you were driving down the road, the open highway, and looked over and found a very little, hard-to-see deer path, that is what the narrow gate is like. You can easily see the devastation and destruction of the broad gate. Satan gives the impression that it's wide open so come on in. But Jesus is the narrow way. When you find that way, it leads to eternal life and greatness. Don't follow the broad gate, which the world wants you to do. Find the narrow gate. Find Jesus and walk in.

Mission

Don't get off the narrow path.

Daily Notes: _____

_____

_____

_____

_____

NATIVE

November 29

Native: being the place or environment in which a person was born or a thing came into being.

Acts 28:7 — *In the same quarters were possessions of the chief man of the island, whose name was Publius; who received us, and lodged us three days courteously.*

Testimony

Paul had three days. What do you think Paul did? He just survived a shipwreck, and he had been stoned and left for dead many times. If I were Paul, I would be ready for a nap! But Paul was out leading others to Christ. He got up and healed many in Jesus' name. The natives from Melita were not kind at first, but then Paul began to show them the healing power of Christ. He healed many on the island. Many came with diseases and were healed in Jesus' name.

Mission

Heal in Jesus' name.

Daily Notes: _____

_____

_____

_____

_____

_____

_____

_____

_____

NOVEMBER

November 30

Reflection of the month of November:

Luke 1:31 — *And, behold, thou shalt conceive in thy womb, and bring forth a son, and shalt call his name JESUS.*

Testimony

Jesus birth, life, and death was and is all for you. Think about and reflect on what that means for you. Jesus was born to die for you. Everything He did was for you and to bring His Father glory. Let everything you do be for the Glory of God, too. Don't live each day for yourself; live it for Jesus! If you're 99% sold out to Christ, reach for 100!

Mission

How are you living today? Be sold out for Jesus.

Daily Notes: _____

_____

_____

_____

_____

_____

_____

_____

_____

_____

_____

DELIVER

December 1

Deliver: to give into another's possession or keeping.

Daniel 6:22 — *My God hath sent his angel, and hath shut the lions mouths, and they have not hurt me: forasmuch as before him innocence was found in me; and also before thee, O king, have I done no hurt.*

Testimony

The world would look at Daniel's situation in the lion's den and say, "Well the lions weren't hungry." This isn't true. When the king called upon Daniel, he said that the Lord sent an angel to shut their mouths. Not only that, but when Daniel came out of the den, the accusers were thrown in, and the lions broke their bones and ate them. God delivered Daniel out of the den. It wasn't a coincident. It wasn't that the lions had a full belly. It was the power and protection of Jesus that delivered Daniel. Just like Jesus delivered Daniel from the den, He will deliver you out of your den. Have you found yourself at your wits ends or do you feel at times like you would love to shut the mouths of those around you? Are you overwhelmed? Daniel called upon the Lord and the Lord shut the mouths of the lions and protected Daniel. Let Jesus deliver you, too. Nothing is impossible for Jesus; He will deliver you from your den.

Mission

If you can't seem to get out of the den you're in right now, pray to Jesus. He will provide a way out. In the meantime, He will shut the mouths of those around you. He will give you peace and protection if you call upon Him.

Daily Notes: _____

DEVOUR

December 2

Devour: swallow or eat up

> **Ezekiel 8:7** — *And he brought me to the door of the court; and when I looked, behold a hole in the wall.*

Testimony

God gave Ezekiel a vision. Ezekiel was standing at the door and got distracted by the hole in the wall. The hole, once you were in it, you were digging and able then to see the wickedness. The hole, and the distraction of it, represents us and how we get distracted by sin. We walk off the path and away from the door that Christ has provided. The bottom line is: don't get distracted by the holes in the wall. The hole might look innocent at first, but it represents sin. Sin takes work. The work of digging the hole is like us working our way through sin. There is nothing easy about living the sinful life. I imagine the top of the hole, before a person starts digging, to look something like this: for an alcoholic it might be a few beers, but once you start digging, you've become an alcoholic, needing it to survive.

Don't give the devil an inch or he will become your ruler, and you will end up digging. Look away from the hole, and look towards the door. Throw down your shovel. Any time temptation arrives, view it as a hole, throw down your shovel and go nowhere near it. Instead, run to the door Christ has provided. He will always provide a way out in the time of temptation.

Mission

Have your mind focused so much on Christ that the holes don't have a chance to devour you.

Daily Notes: _____

DECREASE

December 3

Decrease: to diminish or lessen in extent, quality, or strength.

John 3:30 — *He must increase, but I must decrease.*

Testimony

Who is in charge of your life? Think about your daily activities and routine. What you're doing daily says a lot about who is in control of your life. A blessed life is a life that is controlled by Jesus Christ. If you want blessings, miracles, healing, and peace, stop trying to run your own life. You must decrease so He can increase.

I was chopping strawberries one day and dropped an onion in the bowl. Whatever that onion touched, you could tell it had been there. The bowl was ruined. Not only had I dropped an onion in, but I must have used the knife I had previously used to cut the onion. Now the whole bowl of strawberries smelled like onions. As funny as this story is, it's true in how we want to be consumed with Jesus. Do you want your relationship with the Lord to be like the strawberries or the onion? How much of yourself are you giving to Jesus?

Does He have all of you? Does He have your whole heart? People should be able to look at you and know who you serve. Jesus should be the onion in your life.

Mission

Decrease and be consumed with Jesus.

Daily Notes: _____

_____

_____

_____

_____

DEVOTION

Devotion: profound dedication

John 15:4 — *Abide in me, and I in you. As the branch cannot bear fruit of itself, except it abide in the vine; no more can ye, except ye abide in me.*

Testimony

The vine and the branch need each other to bear fruit. That is the same as our relationship with Christ. We need Jesus because without him we can do nothing. He is the One that we need to be devoted to so our life will bear fruit. The fruit we bear is because of Jesus. When I started writing this devotional book, I knew it had to be something that Jesus wanted me to do. When Jesus confirmed that He wanted me to do this, I became devoted to it. I knew it was something that Jesus would use to bear fruit, just like the vine and the branch.

Mission

Be devoted to Christ. Let Him work amazing things in and through you. When Jesus confirms that He wants you to do something in your life, be devoted to it. Don't quit.

Daily Notes: _____

_____

_____

_____

_____

_____

_____

_____

DEFINE

Define: to explain or identify

1 John 3:1 — *Behold, what manner of love the Father hath bestowed upon us, that we should be called the sons of God: therefore the world knoweth us not, because it knew him not.*

Testimony

If you could define yourself, what would you say about yourself? If someone else would define you, what would they say? The most important thing that we must realize is who Christ says we are. We are sons and daughters of God. You are a child of the King. That is your identity. It should define you. Do not let anyone tell you you're something you're not. If you have accepted Christ as your Savior, you are defined as a Child of the King.

I was shopping at Walmart one night and on the way home the Lord laid on my heart the words, "instant potatoes." It started out as a crazy thing because I couldn't get those potatoes off my mind and it ended up being one of the most amazing "God moments" of my life. I went home and thought, "Who cares? I don't even want these instant potatoes."

I went inside, let my dog out, put my things away, and started to settle down for the evening. I looked at the clock and I start stressing. "I need those potatoes." Normally I am not this type of person, but I kept looking at the clock, stressing about getting to Dollar General Store in time to buy those instant potatoes. I picked up my phone and read some scripture, but nothing was confirmed. I still couldn't shake the feeling that I needed those potatoes. So I got ready, got in the car, and said, "Lord, either I'm crazy or You have a plan for me." I prayed on the way. I pull into the Dollar General Store and a girl that was putting her groceries away said, "Hey Kayla!" I recognized the girl as an acquaintance of mine during my lowest party days. We started talking about the Lord and she told me she was coming to church with me the next day. We said our good byes.

I went into the store saw another girl who used to go to our church. She told me everything that had been going on with her and started to cry. She hugged me and we talked about the Lord.

These two girls were my "instant potatoes." Don't try to define your plans; just go with it. Don't miss out on what God has planned. I could have defined the situation as crazy, but I would have missed out on an amazing "God moment." Let Jesus define you and your situations.

Mission
Redefine yourself with Jesus.

Daily Notes: _____

_____

_____

_____

_____

_____

_____

_____

_____

_____

_____

_____

_____

_____

_____

_____

_____

_____

DECISIONS

December 6

Decisions: act or process of deciding

> **Romans 8:38-39** — _For I am persuaded, that neither death, nor life, nor angles, nor principalities, nor powers, nor things present, nor things to come, nor height, nor depth, nor any other creature, shall be able to separate us from the love of God, which is in Christ Jesus our Lord._

Testimony

Nothing can separate you from the love of God. Isn't that amazing that He loves us that much? He confirms and reaffirms that nothing — I mean nothing — can separate us from the love God has for us! You cannot do anything to make Jesus love you any more or any less than He already does. No decisions you make can make God's love for you change. Make sure you are making decisions that will keep your mind on Jesus because you are always on His! Don't make decisions that will pull you away from God. Instead make decisions that will keep you close and pull you into a deeper relationship with Him.

Mission

Let Jesus make your decisions. He loves you and always has the best decision for you.

Daily Notes: _____

_____

_____

_____

_____

_____

DIFFERENCE

December 7

Difference: the state of being different

> **Luke 15:4** — *What man of you, having an hundred sheep, if he lose one of them, doth not leave the ninety and nine in the wilderness, and go after that which is lost, until he find it?*

Testimony

You may think you're standing out, looking unique, or awkward, but if the difference you're making influences one soul to find Jesus, then it's worth it. This scripture above states that it is. Get out of your comfort zone and make a difference. Be in tune and listen to the Holy Spirit. Sometimes the Holy Spirit will have you do some odd things, but it's for a difference-making moment. He is always changing lives in a positive way. Make a difference to the "one." One is worth it. Be the difference you want to see in the world. If you want to see people saved and serving Christ, then live in a different kind of way, opposite from this world, and make a difference. Don't serve Christ the way your church wants you to or way the world expects you to. Serve Christ the way He wants to be served. Be obedient to the Holy Spirit and make a difference. Jesus is calling you to be a difference maker.

Mission

Be different.

Daily Notes: _____

_____
_____
_____
_____

DOUBT

Doubt: to be uncertain about; consider questionable.

James 1:8 — *A double minded man is unstable in all his ways.*

Testimony

Don't doubt the Lord. He is Lord of all. Stress comes when we doubt that God is able to direct our lives better than we can. My husband and I are in the process of looking for a house. It's been a six month process of searching only to end up in one dead end after another. We have not once doubted that Jesus knows where He wants us and what house He wants us to buy. No matter what the circumstance looks like — or doesn't look like — know the One who is looking at the end of the story, already seeing your future as your past. Don't be unstable. Being unstable in our lives comes when we doubt. Pray and trust in the One who knows all. Let Jesus drive the doubt out of your life by giving Him the wheel.

Mission

Replace doubt and double mindedness with assurance and faith knowing that God is in control of everything.

Daily Notes: _____

_____

_____

_____

_____

_____

_____

DWELL

December 9

Dwell: to reside

Ephesians 3:20 — *Now unto him that is able to do exceeding abundantly above all that we ask or think, according to the power that worketh in us.*

Testimony

Each year my pastor encourages us to pray for Jesus to give us a word to learn about and focus on for the New Year. For the year of 2016 the Lord gave me the word "think." At first my reaction was "Oh no, the Lord wants me to think!" I can remember as a kid my dad saying, "Think about it, Kayla!" My first reaction was, "Oh, I'm in trouble." When I started to study and pray about it, I realized that I had the wrong perspective about the word "think." The Lord loves you and I so much that He just wants us to continuously "think" on Him and His love for us. Think on pure, lovely, praise worthy and pleasant things. The Lord never wants us to dwell or think of negative things or bad things of our past. He loves us so much He wants us to be content, thinking on Him. He is able to do more than we think He can. He is able to do all that we ask or think.

Mission

Think on Jesus.

Daily Notes: _____

_____

_____

_____

_____

DISCIPLE

Disciple: one of the 12 personal followers of Christ and any other professed follower of Christ.

> **Mark 3:14-15** — *And he ordained the twelve, that they should be with him, and that he might send them forth to preach, and to have power to heal sickness, and to cast out devils.*

Testimony

The men Jesus picked to be His disciples were probably not the ones I would have picked. Peter denied him, Thomas was a doubter, and now Jesus picks us! If I were Jesus, I wouldn't have called me to be His disciple. I was partying in bars and living in sin. Why would Jesus pick me? Why does Jesus pick us? Why did He pick those twelve men? He loves us. He loves us so much. He loves us to the point where He looks past our past and sees our potential and our future with Him. He looks at our hearts. He sees our intentions. Jesus doesn't make mistakes. He knew these twelve men were just men. He knew we were just men and women as well, but He also knew that we needed Him. That's why He picked us. Because of Him, we have His Spirit living inside of us. The same Jesus that walked among the twelve men in the Bible is the same Jesus living inside of us. The things the disciples had the power to do, we have the power to do. He is calling you to be a disciple to the world. Will you accept the calling?

Mission

Jesus picked you. Now be a disciple for Him.

Daily Notes: _____

_____

DONE

December 11

Done: past tense of do

> **Mark 5:28** — *For she said, If I may touch but his clothes, I shall be whole.*

Testimony

When she touched his clothes, her faith made her whole. It was done. Jesus did everything He said He would do and it is finished. Whatever you're going through today, know that if you call upon Jesus, it's done. It's over! It's finished! If you reach out and call upon His name, it is finished! Whatever comes to your mind, wherever you are, say to yourself, "It's done!" I am done with this situation. I'm done feeling this way. I'm done having a bad day. It is done because of Jesus. Reach out to Him and be made whole because it's done.

Mission

Reach out to Jesus. Then shout, "It's done!"

Daily Notes: _____

_____

_____

_____

_____

_____

_____

_____

_____

DARKNESS

December 12

Darkness: quality of being dark

> **Genesis 1:16** — *And God made two great lights; the greater light to rule the day, and the lesser light to rule the night: he made the stars also.*

Testimony

God is not only the ruler of the day, but He is the ruler of the night. God controls all and is creator of all. This verse might talk about the sun and the moon, but who is creator of both? In a lot of shows — especially horror movies — everything bad happens at night. We get a scary feeling when we walk into a dark room which is opposite of the brave feeling we get when it's light out. Why is it that darkness gives us such a creepy feeling at times? Be comforted by this truth of this verse: the greater light that rules the day is more powerful than the night. Whatever darkness you feel is shadowing over your life, let Jesus light it up. He is ruler of all — the day and the night. If you have darkness in any areas of your life, pray in the name of Jesus over those areas. Do not let the darkness creep in. If it already has, then in the name of Jesus let it be gone. My favorite saying is, "If you give the devil an inch, he will be come your ruler." Don't let even a little bit of darkness creep into your life. Keep all the darkness away and let your light be bright. Jesus is the light. Put Him in the center of your darkness.

Mission

Light it up.

Daily Notes: _____

_____

_____

DESIRE

December 13

Desire: to wish or long for.

> **Psalm 37:4** — *Delight thyself also in the Lord; and he shall give thee the desires of thine heart.*

Testimony

Trust the Lord with all life's problems. Delight yourself in Him because He will bring it to pass. What is your heart's desires? Do they line up with the Word of God? The Lord will give us the desires of our heart when they match His will for our lives. Why not delight yourself in Him until your desires come to pass? The Lord will not withhold anything good from His children. If you are a parent, would you not give your child something good if you could? That's the way the Lord is with us. He knows our heart's truest desires and He will give them to us. Don't worry; just trust in the Lord. The desires of your heart is coming. In the meantime, delight in Him. Be hopeful and praise His holy name because He is working it all out for your good and His glory.

Mission

Delight for the desire.

Daily Notes: _____

_____

_____

_____

_____

_____

_____

DISCOURAGEMENT

Discouragement: state of being discouraged.

Genesis 3:21 — *Unto Adam also and to his wife did the Lord God make coats of skins, and clothed them.*

Testimony

Talk about discouragement; Adam and Eve had to put together leaves to wear as clothes. All of a sudden, they knew they were naked. Then they hid from the Lord. When confronted by the Lord, they didn't apologize but played the blame game instead. What does God do? He covers them and makes them clothes. They made the mistake. They did wrong, but the Lord made them something better. They covered themselves with leaves; God made them coats. Doesn't that sound a lot like us? We think we have the best plan while God is standing by with a better plan; a coat. God has the best plan for your life. The more of Jesus you have in your life, the more your life will shine.

Mission

Don't stand around with your plan while God is holding a coat for you.

Daily Notes: _____

_____

_____

_____

_____

_____

_____

DAY

December 15

Day: time between sunrise and sunset.

Colossians 3:3 — *For ye are dead, and your life is hid with Christ in God.*

Testimony

My grandfather always quotes this poem, "Only one life soon shall pass; only what's done for God will last." How many days do we let go by and spend no time in prayer, no time with the Lord, no time witnessing, and the whole day is consumed with other things. If our life is hidden in Christ, we have a personal relationship with him and it should be personal. We don't need to go a day without speaking to our wives or husbands. How much more do we need to communicate with the Lord? Everything we do daily that's not for Jesus is temporal and will not last. Make sure each day you're doing something for the Lord. Spend time with the Lord and make an eternal difference everyday.

Mission

Get more personal with Jesus throughout the day.

Daily Notes: _____

_____

_____

_____

_____

_____

_____

_____

DREAM

December 16

Dream: images passing through the mind during sleep.

Matthew 1:20 — *But while he thought on these things, behold, the angel of the Lord appeared unto him in a dream, saying, Joseph, thou son of David, fear not to take unto thee Mary thy wife: for that which is conceived in her is of the Holy Ghost.*

Testimony

A lot of the time we think so much about Mary when we think of Jesus birth — and we should — but what about Joseph? Joseph was also chosen by the Lord to be the earthly father of Jesus. Before even knowing the truth about Jesus, Joseph had plans to put Mary away privately because he didn't want to make her an example. Scripture tells us he was a just man. Can you imagine the feelings Joseph had? Both Joseph and Mary experienced all the human emotions that we can imagine, but then Joseph had a dream. It wasn't some big eye-opening confession, or a big sign, it was simply a dream. Would you have trusted a dream? We can tell Joseph was a wise man because after having the dream, he took Mary as his wife and followed through with God's plan.

So stop looking for some big, jaw-dropping sign. Simply do what God has told you to do. He gave us His Word and told us what to do. Jesus doesn't make things complicated. He is not the author of confusion. Just like He did with Joseph, He will tell us what He wants us to do. It's time to stop day dreaming and do it.

Mission

Don't dream; just do.

Daily Notes: _____

DOCTRINE

December 17

Doctrine: something that is taught.

2 Timothy 3:16 — *All scripture is given by inspiration of God, and is profitable for doctrine, for reproof, for correction, for instruction in righteousness.*

Testimony

The entire Word of God was written by men under the inspiration of the Holy Spirit. All scripture can be used for our good. We are told by Jesus to spread the gospel. This verse is assurance that all scripture is approved by God and can be used for teaching. The Word can be used to correct what has been wrong, teach how to do it right, and then show us how to walk in the righteousness of God. This verse gives us great hope that the Lord always follows through. He doesn't just correct you, tell you what's wrong, and leave you. Because He loves you, He will show you the perfect way to go. This is the great news we need to spread to others. We need to tell others that Jesus loves them and died for them, too. Whatever condition they are in, people need to understand God's love for them.

Mission

Spread the word and live it; that's the best way to love. His Word is profitable for all correction and guidance. It will never come back void.

Daily Notes: _____

_____

_____

_____

_____

DEVIL

Devil: the supreme spirit of evil; satan.

> **Luke 22:31-32** — *And the Lord said, Simon, Simon, behold, Satan hath desired to have you, that he may sift you as wheat: but I have prayed for thee, that thy faith fail not: and when thou art converted, strengthen thy brethren.*

Testimony

Know your enemy. Don't ever think you're strong enough to defeat the devil on your own. His desire is to sift you as wheat, but praise be to God for daily standing in on our behalf. When you're moving closer to the Lord and get to the point where you want to live for Jesus, don't be surprised if something wrong happens or things get a little messy. Instead, be encouraged because the devil knows he is about to lose you and he is just trying to get you back. Turn those stumbling blocks into stepping stones.

I have a small dachshund named Pookie who sat on my lap while I was writing most of this devotional. When I moved just a little bit, she switched her weight to one side. When I moved to the other side, she switched her weight again so she wouldn't fall off. No matter which way I move, Pookie moved, too, trying to hang on no matter what I do.

The devil might try his best to move in front of everything you're trying to do. He might try to block you and stop anything you're trying to do for the Lord, but try is all he can do. Jesus is bigger, greater, and stronger than anything satan can do. Jesus is so powerful that all you have to do is say His name and the demons in hell crawl. Know your enemy, but also know who is in control of the enemy and who is greater. Fight the devil with Jesus and you win every time.

Mission

Just say 'Jesus.'

Daily Notes: _____

DELICIOUS

Delicious: very pleasing; delightful

> **Genesis 3:6** — *And when the woman saw that the tree was good for food, and that it was pleasant to the eyes, and a tree to be desired to make one wise, she took of the fruit thereof, and did eat, and gave also unto her husband with her; and he did eat.*

Testimony

Come on Eve! It wasn't an ice cream tree or a big juicy steak; it was a fruit! I know I'm making light of the situation here but why did Eve eat the fruit? The serpent made it seem delicious. The serpent twisted God's words and made it seem so delicious that she had to have it. The temptation entered her mind when she was around the serpent. If you have problem drinking, don't go to the bar or a party.

Whatever your temptation is, stay away from it and don't listen to the devil. If you're having bad thoughts, they are from satan so get rid of them. Don't entertain the devil. The only thing he will do is tempt you to do the one thing God told you not to do. If you constantly put yourself in a situation where you can be tempted, you will get hurt. Whatever you struggle with, put some distance between yourself and that thing. Don't let satan make you think something is delicious that will kill you. In this case the whole world felt the effects forever. If you give into your temptation the same can be true for you.

Mission

Take control of your thoughts and only listen to Jesus. Get rid of the temptation. It's not delicious!

Daily Notes: _____

DESERVE

December 20

Deserve: have a claim too

Luke 23:34 — *Then said Jesus, Father, forgive them; for they know not what they do. And they parted his raiment, and cast lots.*

Testimony

Do you know how these people were acting? They were mocking Jesus saying, "Crucify Him!" They spit on Him and they beat Him. When He was thirsty, they gave him vinegar to drink. They placed a crown of thorns on His head and nailed His hands and feet to the cross. They whipped Him 39 times across the back — which would have killed most — and how did Jesus respond? He said, "Father forgive them. They know not what they do."

We deserve the death on the cross, but Jesus, in His love for us, endured the cross with us on His mind. Is there a greater love than this? Does a greater love than this exist? It does not exist! It is the greatest love story known throughout history. The best, most amazing part of the story, is that we are part of it. How loved are you? You're loved so much that the Savior of the World took your place — the place you deserved; the death you deserved. Jesus, in His love for you, took your part. Jesus didn't deserve it, but He would do it again just for you.

Mission

Thank Jesus for the undeserving love He gives you daily.

Daily Notes: _____

_____

_____

_____

DAMAGE

December 21

Damage: injury or harm that reduces value or usefulness.

1 Thessalonians 5:17 — *Pray without ceasing.*

Testimony

How important is prayer? Prayer is our direct communication to Jesus. I've heard an old tale that goes, "A family that prays together, stays together." Who is your family? It's whoever accepts Christ as their personal Savior. They are your brothers and sisters in Christ. Needless to say, we all have a big family. Make sure you're praying constantly and in direct communication with Jesus. This keeps your personal relationship with Christ growing. Isn't your church family also your family? Satan wants to tear apart the families and cause great damage in relationships, then there will be no church. Prayer in the name of Jesus stops the enemy, his damage, and his schemes.

Mission

Pray together and stay together. Do this with everyone, everywhere, and all the time. Pray without ceasing.

Daily Notes: _____

_____

_____

_____

_____

_____

_____

DELIGHT

Delight: a high degree of pleasure or enjoyment; joy

1 Thessalonians 5:16 — *Rejoice evermore.*

Testimony

How many times does Jesus need to tell us in His Word to be joyful, delight in Him, and rejoice? It is a constant theme throughout the entire Word of God to rejoice and delight in Him. Even in our trials, Jesus promises us a way out. He will turn our bad into good when we give it over to Him. "Rejoice evermore" has no limitations attached to it. There is no excuse or way out. Jesus says to rejoice evermore. It's simple. Jesus wants us to enjoy life and be happy. If you find yourself in a status of not rejoicing or being delightful, then get out of the world and into the Word.

Mission

Rejoice evermore.

Daily Notes: _____

_____

_____

_____

_____

_____

_____

_____

_____

_____

DARLING

December 23

Darling: one dearly loved

> **Song Of Solomon 4:7** — *Thou art all fair, my love; there is no spot in thee.*

Testimony

Song of Solomon is a love story, one of a strong love which cannot be destroyed. This verse says that he found no spot in her. She was perfection. Isn't it amazing that Christ loves us with that same type of love that cannot be destroyed? There is nothing we can do to make Christ love us more or less. He just loves us. He loves His creation. We weren't perfect when Christ called us into a relationship with Him; and we aren't perfect now that we have a relationship with Him, however, His love for us does not change. He loves you now. He loved you then. He loves you forever more. You are darling to Christ.

Mission

Try to wrap your mind around how much Jesus loves you. Try again. That doesn't even come close to His incomprehensible love. It's so big. Know that you are loved that much.

Daily Notes: _____

_____

_____

_____

_____

_____

_____

DEBTS

Debts: something that is owed

> **Luke 17:15-16** — *And one of them, when he saw that he was healed, turned back, and with a loud voice glorified God, and fell down on his face and at his feet, giving Him thanks: and he was a Samaritan.*

Testimony

Jesus healed ten and only one came back. They weren't in debt to Jesus. They didn't owe him anything, so why did the one come back? The one came back to worship, praise, and thank Christ for his healing and his answered prayer that just took place. How do we act once we are healed by Jesus? Do you find yourself acting like the one; or the nine? Even if He doesn't answer your prayer the way you want it to be answered, know that He does hear you and answers every prayer according to His will. Don't be like the nine that went away. Be the one that came back to thank and praise the Lord. Having faith that the healing is coming even if you haven't seen it yet.

Mission

It's not a debt; it's undeserving grace that we need to thank Him for daily. Be like the one.

Daily Notes: _____

_____

_____

_____

_____

_____

DEMAND

December 25

Demand: claim as a right.

> **Daniel 3:19** — *Then was Nebuchadnezzar full of fury, and the form of his visage was changed against Shadrach, Meshach, and Abed-nego: therefore he spake, and commanded that they should heat the furnace up one seven times more than it was wont to be heated.*

Testimony

Can you imagine the boldness! King Nebuchadnezzar demanded the furnace to be heated so the men could be thrown in. Shadrach, Meshach, and Abed-nego declared to Nebuchadnezzar that their God would deliver them out of his hand. Both demanded something, but only one of them demanded and declared in the name of the Lord. Who won? Because of God's favor, the three men walked out of the furnace. The world will demand your attention, time, or abilities. But if you put Jesus first, He will go before you and prepare the way just like he did for these three men.

Mission

Demand Jesus over all in your life.

Daily Notes: _____

_____

_____

_____

_____

_____

_____

_____

DEDICATED

Dedicated: committed to something

> **Romans 12:4-5** — *For as we have many members in one body, and all members have not the same office: So we being many, are one body in Christ, and every one members of another.*

Testimony

Are you dedicated to serving God? Are you dedicated to your church? If you're switching, moving, or not attending church at all, you need to find a church and get dedicated. Attending church is not necessary to being saved, but it helps you grow in the Lord, showing you how to help others. Jesus went to the temple so we should follow His example and go to church as well. A man in our church always says, "You come to church to get help or give it." It's so true. Be dedicated to the Godly things in your life. Be dedicated to the things that help yourself and others grow in the Lord. Don't dedicate yourself to anything else. Christ is most important in your life; not your job or your family. We need to fully dedicate ourselves to Jesus. After all, He gave you your job and your family! Just make sure when you're dedicating time to those things, you're putting Jesus in the middle of it. Dedicate everything you do to Jesus. People, things and your flesh will let you down; but God never will. Stay dedicated to Him and get yourself out of the way.

Mission

Don't debate, just dedicate.

Daily Notes: _____

DEEP

December 27

Deep: extending far down from the top or surface.

Luke 17:15 — *Lord, have mercy on my son: for he is a lunatick, and sore vexed: for often times he falleth into the fire, and oft into the water.*

Testimony

Honestly, I used to skip this story in the Bible because it frightened me. Can you imagine how the dad felt watching it happen in real life with his son? How could it get any deeper than this? I'm sure the father watched his son throw himself in the deep fire and the deep water and thought, "What will it take?" Then Jesus walked by. He knew Jesus was the answer. Jesus rebuked the devil and he left the child.

Jesus goes on to speak the parable of the mustard seed, being the smallest of all seeds, saying, "If you have faith as small as a mustard seed, you can say unto a mountain 'go' in the name of Jesus and it will move. Nothing shall be impossible unto you." Do you think the father had faith? The demon possession of this boy ended with Jesus giving us incredible scripture on our faith. So instead of being frightened, be thankful that nothing is impossible for Jesus. All we need is faith to fix anything.

Mission

Faith will fix problems in the name of Jesus.

Daily Notes: _____

_____

_____

_____

_____

DEFEATED

December 28

Defeated: to overcome in a contest, election, or battle.

Hosea 3:2 — *So I bought her to me for fifteen pieces of silver, and for an homer of barley, and an half homer of barley.*

Testimony

A woman at our church did an incredible job teaching this story. She compared God to Hosea and us to Gomer in the story. In this verse, Gomer turned away from her husband and went back to adultery, the previous life she had lived. Then we see her husband — because of his love for her and his devotion to God — redeem her. Gomer had sunk so far down that she was only worth half the price of a slave, yet God wanted her. Tears stung my eyes as I read about how defeated Gomer must have felt. She was below the status of a slave. To the world, Gomer wasn't even worth the cost of the barley that fed the animals.

God loves you so much. He is your "Hosea." He paid the price and defeated sin for you. Just like Hosea redeemed Gomer, Jesus wants to redeem you. Let Him take you out of whatever mental, physical, or emotional battle you are in and redeem you. If you have accepted Christ and have been redeemed, thank Him for redeeming you at your lowest point. He redeemed you when you were lost, like Gomer, in sin. Run to Him because you are redeemed.

Mission

Don't be defeated. Rely on the fact that you are redeemed. The price has been paid. Jesus didn't die and rise again for us to go around acting defeated. You are an overcomer.

Daily Notes: _____

_____

_____

DEFENDER

December 29

Defender: to ward off attack from

1 Samuel 19:18 — *So David fled, and escaped and came to Samuel to Ramah, and told him all that Saul had done to him. And he and Samuel went and dwelt in Naioth.*

Testimony

God was constantly David's defender. Saul would go one way to kill David and God would direct David the opposite way to defend himself. God always protected David. God placed Jonathan in David's life which also helped David in every way. Jesus is your defender. He will let nothing harm you. He will protect you. Fight your battles on your knees. You will win with Jesus; but you will lose without Him.

Mission

Let Jesus go before you. He is your defender.

Daily Notes: _____

_____

_____

_____

_____

_____

_____

_____

_____

_____

DELAY

December 30

Delay: to put off to a later time

Deuteronomy 28:8 — *The Lord shall command the blessings upon thee in thy store houses, and in all that thou settest thine hand unto; and he shall bless thee in the land which the Lord thy God giveth thee.*

Testimony

Our Grandma Barbara always says, "The Lord has a storage building full of blessings waiting on us." Well, what are we waiting for? Why would we delay blessings from the Lord? Are we too scared to get uncomfortable or stand up for Christ? Don't delay the blessings God has for you anymore. If you're breathing, the Lord wants to bless you! Stop making it complicated. Get into a position where God can easily pour out blessings on you. He wants to do that.

Mission

Don't delay anymore.

Daily Notes: _____

_____

_____

_____

_____

_____

_____

_____

DECEMBER

December 31

Reflection of the month of December. Reflection of your previous year, getting ready to go into the New Year:

> **Philippians 3:13** — *Brethren, I count not myself to have apprehended: but this one thing I do, forgetting those things which are behind, and reaching forth unto those things which are before.*

Testimony

A year ago I wrote a note — before I ever started this devotional — that said, "Read when in need of encouragement." One year later after finishing, I realized I had never had to open it up and read it. Why? Because Jesus wrote it. He did it all for me and through me; I was just willing. So let's be willing this New Year; willing to do whatever Jesus tells us to do. Be willing to say, "Whatever you want from me, Jesus...I am ready!" Be willing! Go! Send me Jesus! Here I am! Go! Go! Go! In the name of Jesus, be willing and go! Get in the will of God!

Mission

Be willing. It starts with you! GO!

Daily Notes: _____

_____

_____

_____

_____

_____

_____

_____

Author Biography

I am a child of God, which you will figure out through reading this devotional. This means everything to me. My name is Kayla Hayhurst. I live in West Virginia. I love the mountains, seasons, and outdoor activities. I am married to a Jesus-loving man. We have a small dachshund named Pookie. We plan on having children one day when the Lord blesses us with them, and we will raise them to walk in the truth and love Jesus. We sponsor a little girl named Asia through World Vision, uplifting her in prayer. My desire is to teach, grow, and live daily in the Word. I use my Facebook and social media networks to help spread the gospel. My goal in life is for people to look at me and see Jesus.